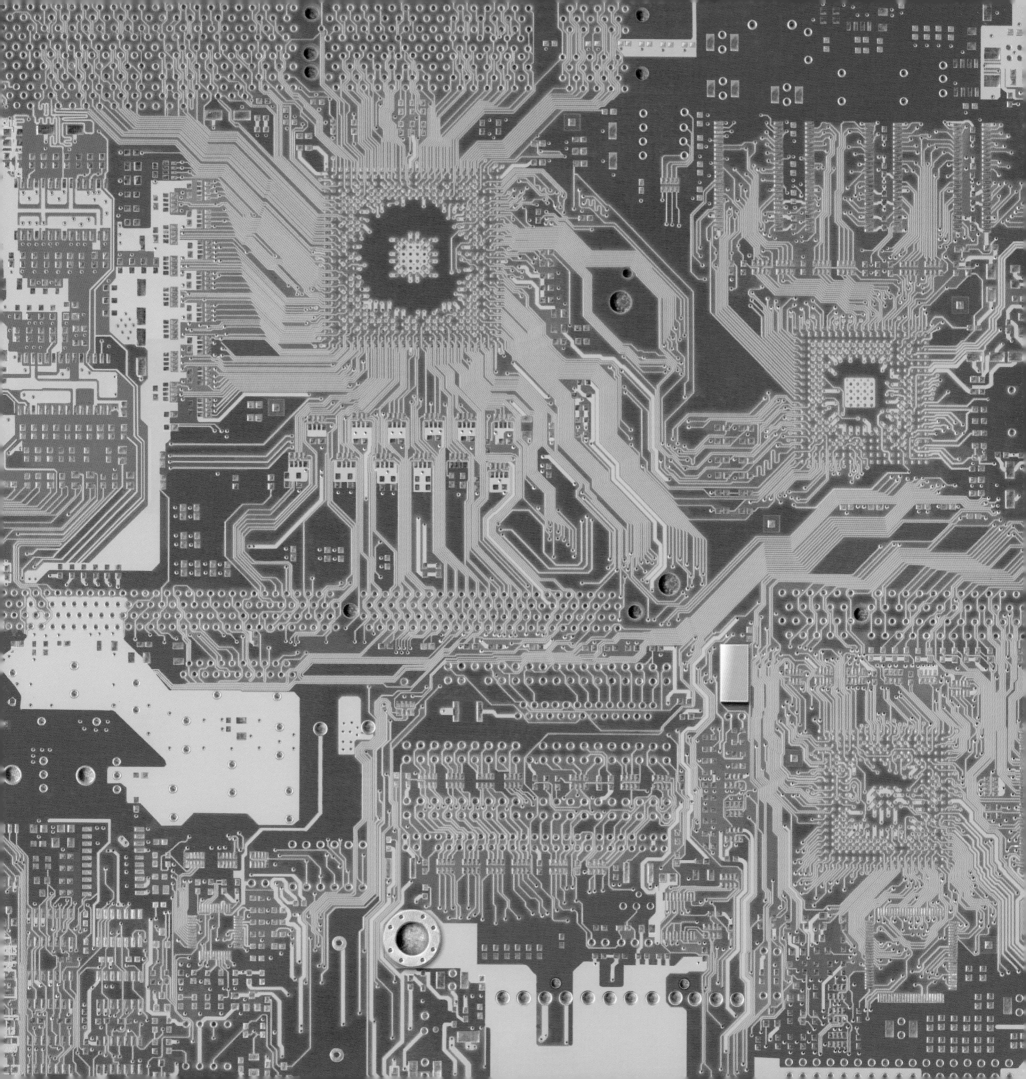

Published in 2005 by Carlton Books Limited
An imprint of the Carlton Publishing Group
20 Mortimer Street
London W1T 3JW

A catalogue record for this book is available from the British Library.

ISBN 1 84442 459 6

Art Director: **Clare Baggaley**
Design: **Simon Wilder simon@shinydesign.demon.co.uk**
Executive Editor: **Stella Caldwell**
Picture Research: **Steve Behan**
Production: **Lisa Moore**

Printed and bound in China

THE COMPUTER

MARK FRAUENFELDER

CARLTON
BOOKS

8

INTRODUCTION

CONTENTS

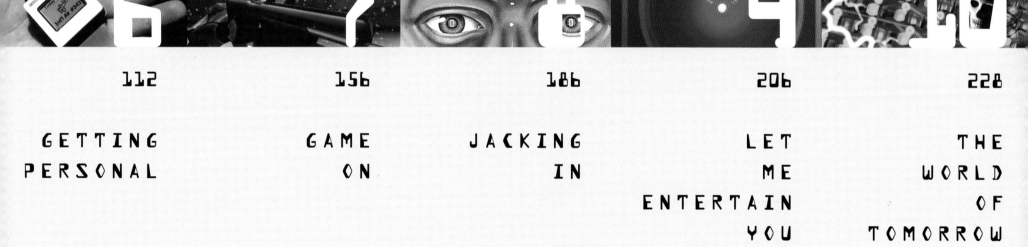

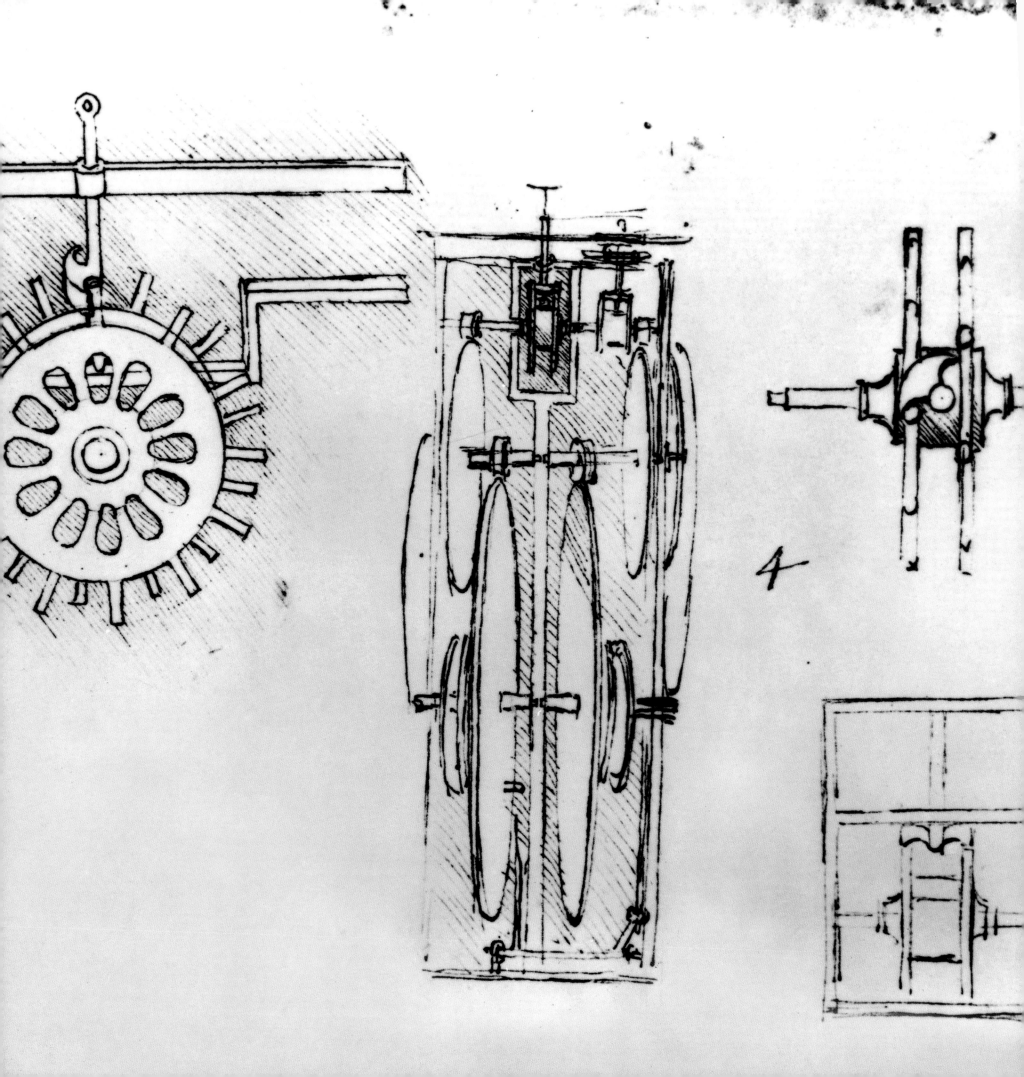

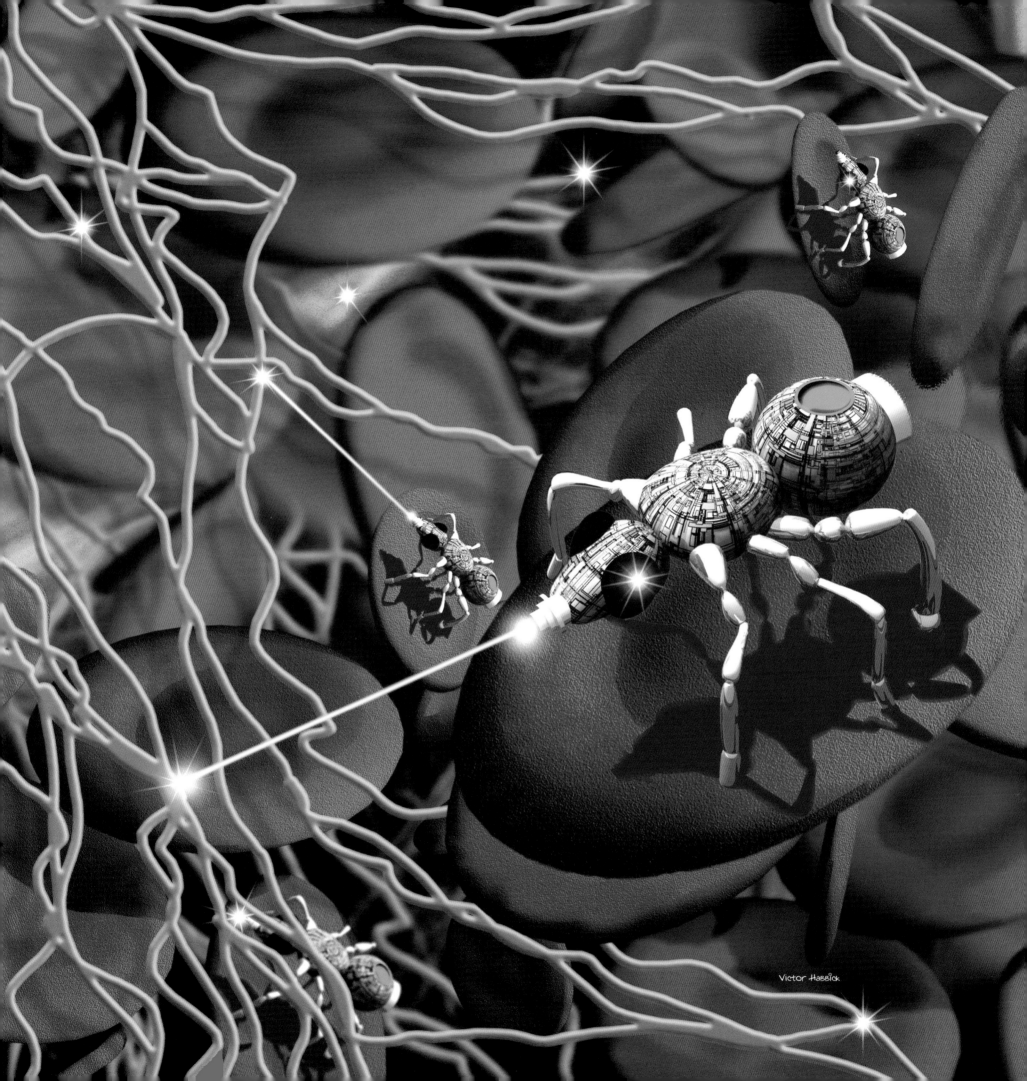

Victor Habbick

To see how far computers have come, perhaps it's best first to look at how far they haven't come.

In the October 1950 issue of the scholarly journal *Mind*, a man named Alan Turing described the rules for a strange game he had invented. The journal would never have published the paper, if it were not for the fact that Turing had contributed more to the development of modern computing than any person in history. He was a British mathematician and had invented a design for a programmable computer. All computers used today are Turing machines.

Turing called his game the Imitation Game. There are three players – one of them must be a man, another must be a woman. It doesn't matter if the third player, the interrogator, is a man or a woman.

The players enter separate rooms, each of which contains a chair and a teleprinter. The interrogator doesn't know which room the man is in and which room the woman is in. It is up to the interrogator to figure that out by typing questions into the teleprinter. It would be easy enough for the interrogator to type "What is your gender?" and wait for the other two players to enter their answers on the teleprinter. But in this game, the man must do everything he can to try to convince the interrogator that he is a woman, while the woman must be completely honest when answering.

At this point, Turing proposes a switcheroo. The man is to leave the room and be replaced with a computer. What happens then, he asks? Will the interrogator decide wrongly as often when the game is played like this as he does when the game is played between a man and a woman?

The reason Turing came up with the Imitation Game (now known as the Turing Test) was to explore the possibility of computers that could one day think (or at least appear to think) well enough to fool the interrogator as often as a person playing the game could fool the interrogator.

Turing had faith in computers. In a paper he wrote: "I believe that in about 50 years' time it will be possible to programme computers with a storage capacity of about 10^9 to make them play the imitation game so well that an average interrogator will not have more than a 70 per cent chance of making the right identification after five minutes of questioning."

Let's fast forward 54 years to the Loebner Prize Turing Test Contest, held every year since 1991. An American inventor and philanthropist, Hugh Loebner – in association with the National Science Foundation and the Sloan Foundation – offers a US$100,000 prize to anyone who can write a computer programme that passes the Turing Test. In 2004 Richard Wallace was awarded US$2,000 and a bronze medal for "the most human computer".

How good was Wallace's programme at fooling the judges? Go ahead and judge for yourself. Here's the beginning of transcripts of conversations between interrogators and players. Try to guess which one is the computer and which one is the human.

CONVERSATION A

Alice: Hello, my name is Alice and I am the human.

Judge: Hi Alice. How are you doing?

Alice: Hello there. Everything is going extremely well.

Judge: I'm glad to here [sic] it. Where do you live?

Alice: Thanks for the information. My location is New York City. Where are you?

Judge: In New York. How did you get here today?

Alice: Tell me a little about your life in New York. Ah. Everything I need to know, I learned from my Instructor.

Judge: Why don't you answer my question first?

Alice: Don't you know? No, I do not answer your question first. Do you? I answer a lot of silly questions.

CONVERSATION B

David: Hello, my name is David and I am the human.

Judge: Hi, I'm Roy. Are you a Yankees fan?

David: Yes, but only because I'm a New Yorker. Generally, I don't follow sports.

Judge: What about art?

David: What about it?

Judge: Is it something that interests you?

David: Yes. I like art very much. Do you?

Judge: Yes, expecially [sic] early modern. Are you familiar with Modegliani [sic]?

David: Yes. I like his work. As far as painting is concerned, I like Juan Gris and the surrealists. Sounds like a band name. I also like... who's the guy who covered the canvas with squares of colour in long lines? He was famous for painting the spirit of jazz, I think.

So, is Alice the computer, or is David? It's not hard to tell. Not a single judge was fooled by Wallace's computer. In fact, none of the entries in the Loebner contest has ever fooled a judge since the contest began. And at the rate at which the field of artificial intelligence is moving, it's not likely that anyone will be taking home the solid gold Loebner medal soon.

Turing was an undisputed polymathic genius who not only laid the foundation for the entire field of computer science but also made significant contributions in the fields of chemistry, biology and physics. How could he have been so far off the mark?

The answer is that a brain is a lot less like a computer than most people originally thought. Science fiction and the media of the 1950s liked to portray computers as "electronic brains" or "thinking machines" that would replace teachers, composers, judges and juries, and other roles that required a human mind to fulfil.

A better analogy is to think of a computer as a bicycle. On an episode of the science television programme *Nova*, Steve Jobs, the co-founder of Apple Computer, marvelled at the way in which a bicycle could transform a slow-moving, easily tired human into a super-efficient traveller able to outrun a cheetah, the world's fastest mammal. A computer, said Jobs, is a "bicycle for the mind". In other words, a computer without a user is like a bicycle without a rider – a machine that doesn't do anything. It needs a human mind to make it work.

The story of computers, therefore, is the story of our relationship with computers: how we think of them, develop them, use them and learn to live in the world we've co-created with them.

The story of computers could be told by describing the advances in memory, speed, miniaturization and so on, but that would only be half the story – the boring half. The more interesting side of computer history is about the people who made computers and software. People like Frenchman Blaise Pascal, a guilt-racked homosexual inflamed with religious fanaticism, who also happens to have made hugely significant contributions to the advancement of mathematics, philosophy and physics before dying of stomach cancer at the age of 39. Or like another guilt-racked homosexual, the aforementioned Alan Turing, who, after helping to save Britain in the Second World War by devising a German code-breaking machine, was charged by an astonishingly ungrateful government with the crime of being gay. He lost his security clearance and was coerced into taking regular oestrogen injections to "cure" him of being gay. In shame, Turing committed suicide by taking a bite out of a poisoned apple.

Speaking of apples, there's a story about the two Steves – Jobs and Wozniak – that reads like a Greek tragedy. In 1976 Steve Jobs was working as a technician at Atari, the famous arcade video game company that made the hit game Pong. Nolan Bushnell, Atari's flamboyant founder, asked Jobs to design the circuitry for a new game Atari was developing, called Breakout. Jobs, who was unable to design complex circuitry, accepted the assignment and turned to his friend, Steve Wozniak, to do the job, promising him half of the US$700 fee Atari was willing to pay. Wozniak and Jobs stayed up four nights straight developing the circuit. They were both so exhausted that they caught mononucleosis, but they met the deadline and Atari paid them.

Jobs and Wozniak later went on to launch Apple Computer, maker of personal computers that had fanatically enthusiastic users. By 1984, with the company flying high and both men rich beyond their dreams, the marathon Breakout design session had been all but forgotten. But on a plane trip to Florida, Wozniak had a conversation with Apple engineer Andy Hertzfeld, who told Wozniak about a book on Atari he was reading, entitled *Zap!* The book, said Hertzfeld, claimed that Jobs alone had designed Breakout. Wozniak said: "I explained to [Hertzfeld] that we both worked on it and got paid $700. Andy corrected me: 'No, it says here it was $5,000.' When I read in the book how Nolan Bushnell had actually paid Steve $5,000, I just cried."

The business of making computers can drive people to tears, but the business of making things with computers can drive them to other emotional, and even transcendental, heights. In the nineteenth century a gifted amateur mathematician and philosopher named Lady Ada Lovelace, the abandoned daughter of Lord Byron, wrote about the almost infinite potential of the Difference Engine, Charles Babbage's Victorian-era, steam-driven computer. A time in which calculating machines were almost unheard of, Lovelace described how a difference engine "might compose elaborate and scientific pieces of music of any degree of complexity or extent", generate sophisticated graphics and generally "do whatever we know how to order it to perform". And she was right. Today, computers are essential tools for the creation of music, movies, games and other forms of art. Sometimes, it's the computers themselves taking starring roles – who can forget the paranoid, murderous HAL from *2001: A Space Odyssey*, or the computer-world villains in *The Matrix*?

HAL is exactly the kind of computer that Alan Turing imagined we might see in the year 2001. The fact that we haven't and yet continue to ascribe the power of thought to computers (at least in movies and novels) reveals something about the mystery of computers and our own sense of what it means to be alive. In some ways, computers do seem to function like the human brain – and we have the urge to bestow them with a quasi-human status.

The alternative is to state that people are machines – fantastically sophisticated ones to be sure – but no more or less special than the computers we've made. And most scientists will tell you that people are nothing more than machines; that free will is an illusion, an epiphenomenon of a universe-sized physics experiment winding down in accordance with the second law of thermodynamics.

Could it be true? That's a question no one can answer with certainty. What is certain is that our relationship with our silicon soulmates will undoubtedly become more intimate in the future. As the average age of people in industrialized nations creeps upward, our greying population will come to depend on computers as caretakers, medicine dispensers and entertainers. The market for domestic robots – home computers with arms and legs – is forecast to explode in the coming years, mainly because the young will be too busy to take care of the elderly. Japan and Korea are already experimenting with "care-bots" that attend to the needs of their senior citizens, monitoring their vital signs and sending emails to the doctor when something is amiss. Studies in these countries have shown that the people being cared for by robots become emotionally attached to their electronic helpers, and consider them to be caring, loving friends. (Maybe the Loebner competition should have a contest for computers that make people feel good.)

The aim of this book isn't to teach you how to design and build your own computer. (There are already plenty of books available that will show you how.) The aim is to give you an insight into the people throughout the centuries who have dedicated their lives to making a technology that touches us all.

DIGITAL DAWN
DIGITAL DAWN
DIGITAL DAWN
DIGITAL DAWN
DIGITAL DAWN
DIGITAL DAWN
DIGITAL DAWN
DIGITAL DAWN
DIGITAL DAWN
DIGITAL DAWN
DIGITAL DAWN
DIGITAL DAWN
DIGITAL DAWN
DIGITAL DAWN
DIGITAL DAWN
DIGITAL DAWN
DIGITAL DAWN
DIGITAL DAWN
DIGITAL DAWN
DIGITAL DAWN
DIGITAL DAWN
DIGITAL DAWN
DIGITAL DAWN
DIGITAL DAWN
DIGITAL DAWN
DIGITAL DAWN
DIGITAL DAWN
DIGITAL DAWN
DIGITAL DAWN

"There is no inquiry which is not finally reducible to a question of numbers" – Auguste Comte

Our early ancestors didn't know how to count. They had a sense of quantity – "There's a lot of fruit in that tree" – but they didn't have a means to express it. That changed one day, tens of thousands of years ago, when an especially smart simian realized she could make a one-to-one correspondence between her fingers and some group of things of which she needed to keep track.

Eventually, when the need arose to account for groups of things that exceeded the numbers of fingers and toes people had, people invented tallies – scratches in the dirt, paint daubs on rock walls and notches in bones. Tallies had the added benefit of being permanent records. At this point in time (around 30,000 BC), people developed the idea of a number as an abstract concept. "Each notch in my bone represents the number of potatoes we saved to eat last winter. I need to save the same number of potatoes for the coming winter."

Later, people gave different names to different numbers of the notches, and after that came the great leap forward of adding, subtracting, multiplying and dividing the numbers. With the introduction of agriculture, arithmetic became indispensable. Humankind's first civilizations – bustling with manufacturing, trade and taxes – were breeding grounds for early computation aids, such as counting boards and abacuses. Ancient Roman engineers and architects used pocket abacuses to design their famous aqueducts and architecture. The abacus moved eastwards to China, and to the rest of the old world. In South America the Incas encoded numbers and other information by tying knots on to arrangements of coloured string. Numbers were as much a part of humankind as language. They became indispensable for navigation, calendars, astronomy, commerce and science.

As a result of becoming more numerate, people became more technologically adept. And as their technology advanced, so did their ability – and need – to process numbers. Take, for example, the Antikythera Device. It was discovered inside a sunken trading ship from 80 BC off the isle of Antikythera, Greece. When scientists began studying it in detail, in the late 1950s, they realized that the corroded brass device, housed in a wooden cabinet, was an astonishingly intricate mechanism that had been used to calculate planetary motion for navigation. Featuring a sophisticated differential gear train (an invention that didn't show up again until 1575, in a globe clock designed by Jobst Bürgi) and closely meshing parts, the device gave archaeologists newfound respect for the technological prowess of the ancient Mediterraneans. John Gleave in the UK recently built a working replica of the device.

After John Napier (1550–1617) invented the logarithm, which transformed the difficult task of multiplying large numbers into the much easier one of adding numbers, inventors began producing machines that could perform numerical calculations for them. The intention was to free their inventors to focus on problems better suited for human minds, such as analyzing the answers delivered by their calculators and making decisions based on them. But these early devices – Schickard's calculating clock, Pascal's adder, Leibniz's stepped reckoner – were too far ahead of their time to have much immediate impact. It was possible for a craftworker painstakingly to make the devices, one at a time, but the manufacturing technology of the era simply wasn't up to snuff. This was, after all, centuries before the Industrial Revolution, with its assembly lines and steam-powered machinery. And so the calculators built during this time either never made it past the prototype stage or were filigreed brass and mahogany treasures for the curiosity cabinets of the wealthy.

These early computing pioneers' dream of creating a tool that would be in every office wouldn't be realized until the methods of manufacture caught up with their genius. In 1820 Frenchman Charles Xavier Thomas de Colmar (1785–1870) invented the Arithmometer, which used many of the same mechanical innovations found in the Leibniz calculator, but it was much more robust, smaller and user-friendly. The low-priced device (about US$150 in today's money) was so reliable that 100 years later the Arithmometer was being produced using essentially the same mechanism as in Thomas's original design. It also led the way for countless imitators and innovators to produce calculators in mass quantities for the burgeoning banking, engineering, manufacturing and insurance industries. The age of mechanical calculating as necessity – rather than novelty – had arrived.

But a calculator isn't a computer, in the same way that a wheel isn't a cart. It's only part of a much more complex machine, one that can store information and process it according to programmed instructions. Progress requires the mind-numbing work of endless number crunching, and that requires a machine that can tirelessly and quickly perform great volumes of tedious arithmetic. But before that could happen, there were many remaining things to be discovered, such as Boolean algebra and the concept of storing information on holes punched in cards.

The next time you sit down in front of your three-pound laptop computer to watch video clips, download music or send email around the planet, give thanks to the first cave dwellers who sawed an obsidian blade across a wolf's jawbone to make a notch. These people made your computer possible.

Earliest known tallying system

Early Cro-Magnon people probably used tallies to keep track of supplies. These notched bones, discovered in Czechoslovakia in 1937, are between 20,000 and 30,000 years old and are the earliest surviving evidence of a tallying system that has been used extensively throughout the centuries. Merchants used wooden tally sticks to indicate how many of a particular item their customers bought. The merchant would split the stick vertically and give one piece to the customer, so that when the bill came, there'd be no arguing over how many casks of oil or loaves of bread had been purchased.

Ur and the counting board

Founded around 3500 BC in Sumer (now Iraq), Ur was the world's first city. Civilization is both a cause and effect of trade and commerce, and both require a lot of arithmetic to keep them running. Ur was likely to have been the birthplace of the counting board, which is like an abacus but without wires holding the beads. Instead, beads or tokens are placed in grooves carved into the counter. One row represents ones, the adjacent row represents tens, and so on. The earliest counting boards were probably not boards at all, but merely furrows scratched in the ground, into which pebbles were placed. In 1899 a Babylonian counting board from 300 BC was discovered on Salamis Island. It is the oldest surviving example of a counting board.

A pocket abacus to build Rome

Even the simplest mathematical operations are very difficult to perform using Roman numerals, so

the engineers and architects who designed the highly complex aqueduct system and buildings

of ancient Rome relied on pocket abacuses to assist them in their calculations. The most common

design was a metal plate with a number of parallel grooves in which beads could be slid and

moved from one groove to another. Each groove represented a different power of 10,

serving as a natural extension of counting on 10 fingers.

Old habits die hard

In many parts of Asia, and in different "Chinatowns" around the world, some shopkeepers and merchants continue to use abacuses for calculating purchases. An experienced user can perform calculations on an abacus with blazing speed. On 12 November 1946 the US Army newspaper *Stars and Stripes* sponsored a contest in Tokyo that pitted an abacus expert named Kiyoshi Matsuzaki, who was from the Savings Bureau of the Ministry of Postal Administration, against an electric calculator operated by Private Thomas Nathan Wood of General MacArthur's 20th Finance Disbursing Section. The competition included adding 50 two- and three-digit numbers, multiplying five- to twelve-digit numbers and various composite problems. Matsuzaki and his abacus beat Wood and his calculator in four out of five categories.

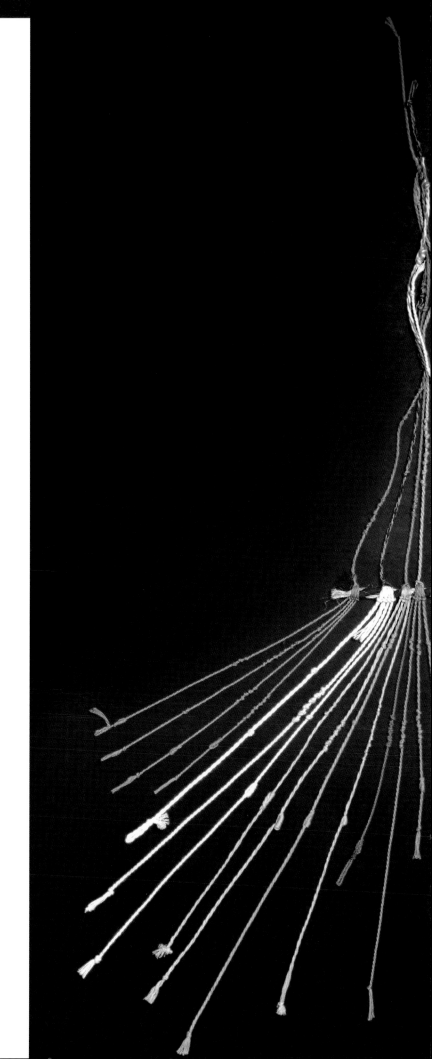

Eratosthenes (c276–c195 BC) was a Greek mathematician of remarkable talent. While living in northern Africa, he came up with an ingenious method to determine the circumference of the Earth, which involved measuring the length of shadows cast at different points when the sun was at its zenith and applying geometry to calculate the result. His answer was within 15 per cent of the Earth's actual circumference. He is also credited with inventing an algorithm (a step-by-step set of instructions for solving a maths problem) to generate prime numbers. Known as the "Sieve of Eratosthenes", the procedure works like this: write a series of whole numbers on a sheet of paper, starting with 2; strike a line through every second number following 2 (thus filtering out all the numbers divisible by 2); strike a line through every third number following 3 (which eliminates all numbers divisible by 3); because 4 is already crossed out, you can ignore it and move on to 5 (which eliminates all numbers divisible by 5). By continuing this algorithm, you can methodically discover the prime numbers – they're the ones that aren't crossed out. Like all algorithms, the Sieve of Eratosthenes is automatic and requires no "thought" to perform. And because computers can't think, algorithms are an essential part of computer programmes.

← ↑ The Quipa (or quipu) was used by ancient South American Indians as a kind of memory storage device. Made from groups of knotted, multi-coloured strings, the quipa's particular twists, knot types, knot positions and string groupings conveyed information that a trained quipa user could understand. While the exact encoding logic of quipas isn't known, it's thought that quipas were used to calculate numbers, to record laws and to retain lore and poetry. The Incas, known for their meticulous record-keeping, used quipas extensively to transmit messages from one place to another. Quipa makers were employed to encode and decode the signals, in the same way that telegraph operators were used in later centuries.

Leonardo da Vinci's mechanical calculator

The quintessential Italian Renaissance man, Leonardo da Vinci (1452–1519), is nearly as famous for his ingenious inventions as he is for his works of art, but it wasn't until 1967 that he was also credited with the invention of the first mechanical calculator. On 13 February of that year, a team of American researchers studying at Madrid's National Library of Spain came across some long-forgotten codices written by Leonardo. In these pages was a drawing of a mechanical calculator that consisted of 13 gears, each of which registered digits from one to 10. As a gear went from 9 to 0, the adjacent gear would advance by one digit. In 1968 IBM commissioned Leonardo expert Roberto Guatelli to build a working model. The model was exhibited to the public, but it was later withdrawn after critics complained that it had been made incorrectly.

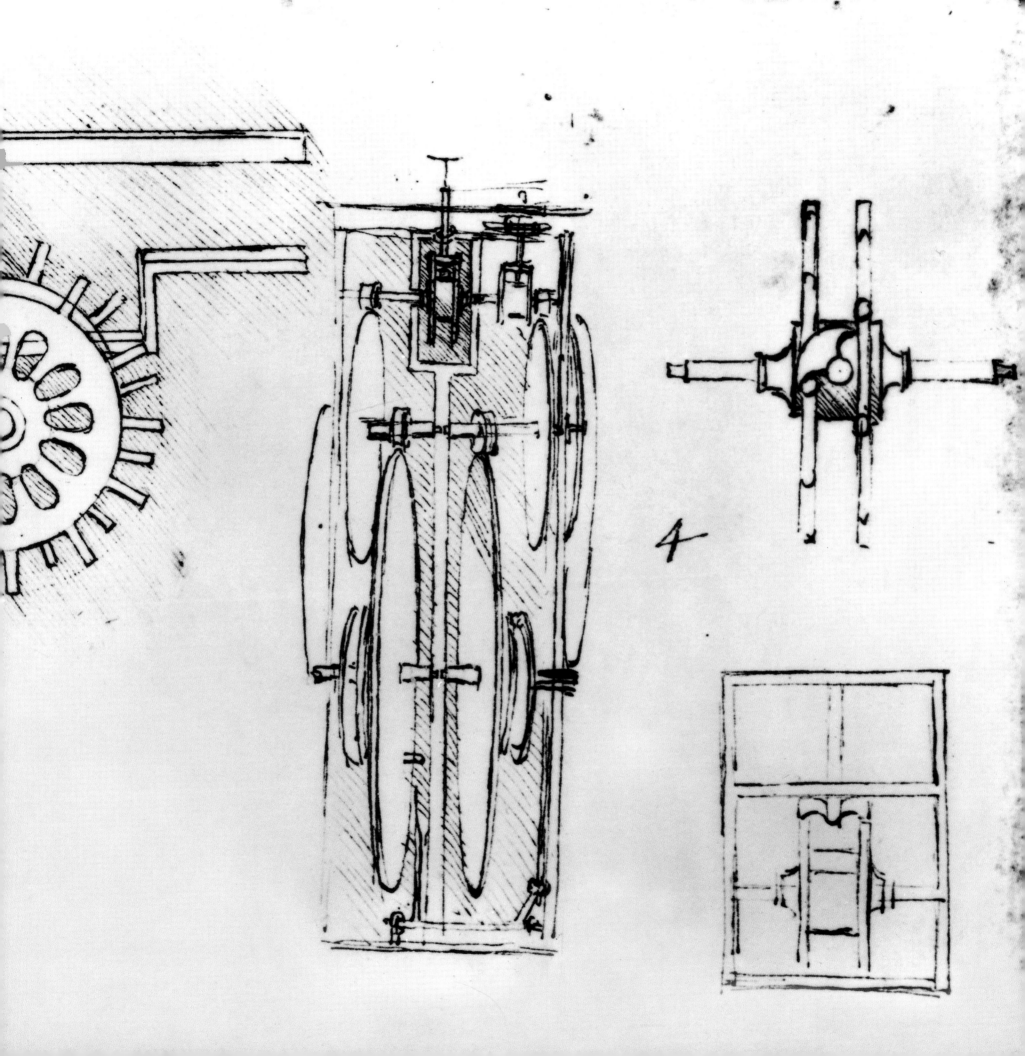

4

John Napier

John Napier (1550–1617), Laird of Merchiston, Scotland, considered himself first and foremost a leader against Catholicism. But today, his lengthy attack against the Pope, *Plaine Discovery of the Whole Revelation of St John* (1593), which he believed was his most important contribution to humanity, is largely forgotten, while his discovery of logarithms remains one of the greatest mathematical achievements of all time. Logarithm tables can be used to convert multiplication and division to simple addition and subtraction. His invention was of tremendous benefit to the advancement of astronomy, cartography, geometry and navigation.

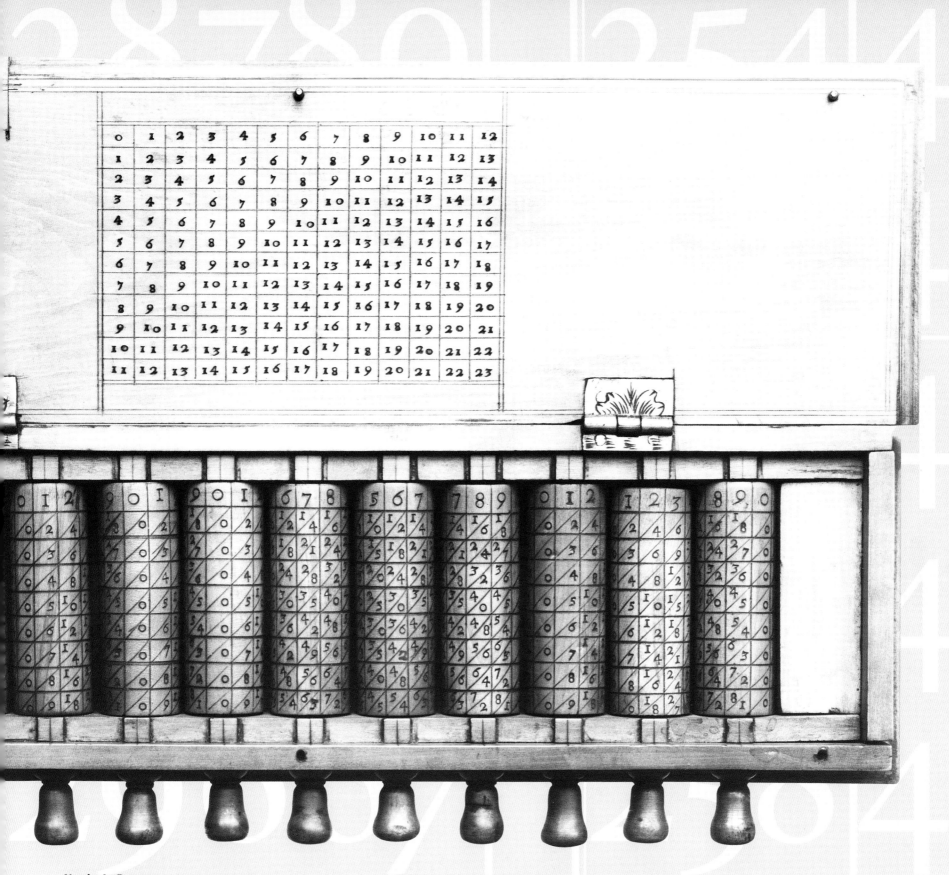

Napier's Bones

Shortly before he died, Napier invented a set of sticks that incorporated the logarithmic tables. Known as Napier's Bones or Napier's Rods, the sticks were inscribed with numerals and could be placed next to each other in such a way as to multiply large numbers. Napier's Bones were a huge hit in Europe, where even educated people were mathematically challenged. The most expensive sets were made from ivory and came in leather boxes. Later refinements included rotating cylinders mounted on axles, as shown here. As Hindu-Arabic maths made its way across the European continent in later years, Napier's Bones eventually become obsolete.

William Oughtred

The slide rule, which uses logarithmic scales to perform mathematical operations, was invented by William Oughtred (1574–1660). As a rector in Albury, Surrey, England, Oughtred was a keen amateur mathematician and taught maths to the local youngsters. In 1630 one of his students, Richard Delamain, published a paper that laid claim to the invention of the slide rule. Oughtred and Delamain argued bitterly for years over who had actually come up with the idea. It's now thought that Delamain, while the first to publish the idea, invented it independently after Oughtred. Slide rules were in common use until the mid-1970s, when they were replaced by electronic pocket calculators. One of Oughtred's inventions remains with us today, however: the use of "X" to indicate multiplication.

Wilhelm Schickard

Wilhelm Schickard (1592–1635), a Lutheran minister from Germany, was a genius who excelled in many fields. He was fluent in Hebrew and Aramaic, and studied astronomy, mathematics and cartography. He was also a brilliant inventor and devised machines for Hebrew grammar and astronomy. In 1623 Schickard invented what he called a Calculating Clock, arguably the first mechanical calculator. He was unable to make more than one, however, because the 30 Years' War was taking its toll on most of Europe. Famine and disease, which wiped out nearly half of Germany, also claimed Wilhelm Shickard and he died of the plague in 1635.

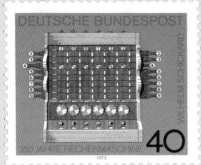

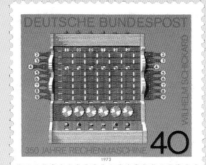
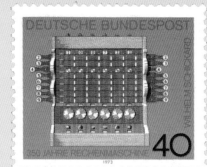

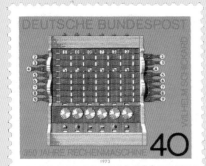

Shickard's Calculating Clock

Shickard's Calculating Clock was forgotten until 1935, when an historian

named Franz Hammer found Shickard's small drawing of it at Pulkovo

Observatory near St Petersburg, Russia. In 1957 Hammer found another

drawing of the machine, along with instructions for making it. He presented

his findings at a maths history conference and one of the attendees, Dr Bruno

Baron von Freytag, took it upon himself to build a working model in 1960. In

1973 the German post office celebrated the 350th anniversary of Shickard's

Calculating Clock with this postage stamp.

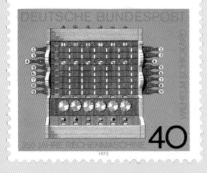

←| The Pascaline

The 19-year-old Blaise Pascal invented his adding machine, known as the Pascaline, in 1642, to help his tax collector father figure accounts. The Pascaline enjoyed tremendous fame throughout Europe, but rather than being a workhorse number cruncher, it was mainly a rich man's parlour curiosity. Only about a dozen were actually sold and the finicky device was prone to jamming.

|→ Blaise Pascal

Before he succumbed to stomach cancer at the age of 39, the extraordinary Blaise Pascal (1623–1662) wrote a seminal essay on solid geometry (at the age of 16), discovered the fundamentals of fluid physics, invented the hydraulic press and the syringe, contributed to the establishment of probability theory and developed the modern French prose style. While he is considered by many to have invented the first adding machine, Wilhelm Schickard actually holds that honour.

Morland's adder

Samuel Morland (1625–1695), a diplomat for Cromwell, spent the later years of his life inventing. He built a steam engine in the basement of his house, which he had leased from the Duchy of Cornwall. He invented what was arguably the first internal combustion engine (a water pump that burned gunpowder). He also invented a mechanized version of Napier's Bones, a megaphone, two types of barometer, a device for trigonometry calculations and a machine that could add old-style (£/s/d) currency. While his adder incorporated some unusual and clever features, it also had problems and was not practical. After Samuel Pepys saw it in 1667, he wrote in his diary that Morland's adder was "very pretty but not very useful".

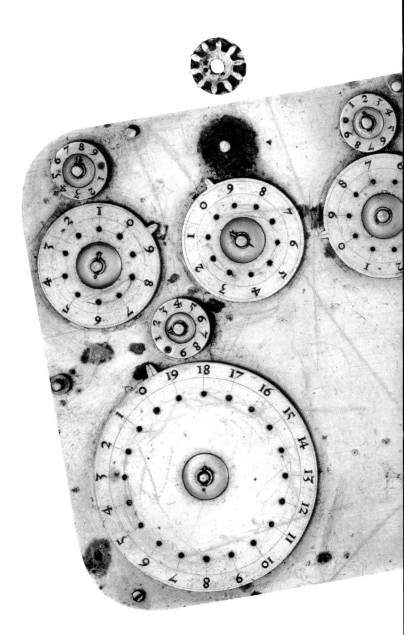

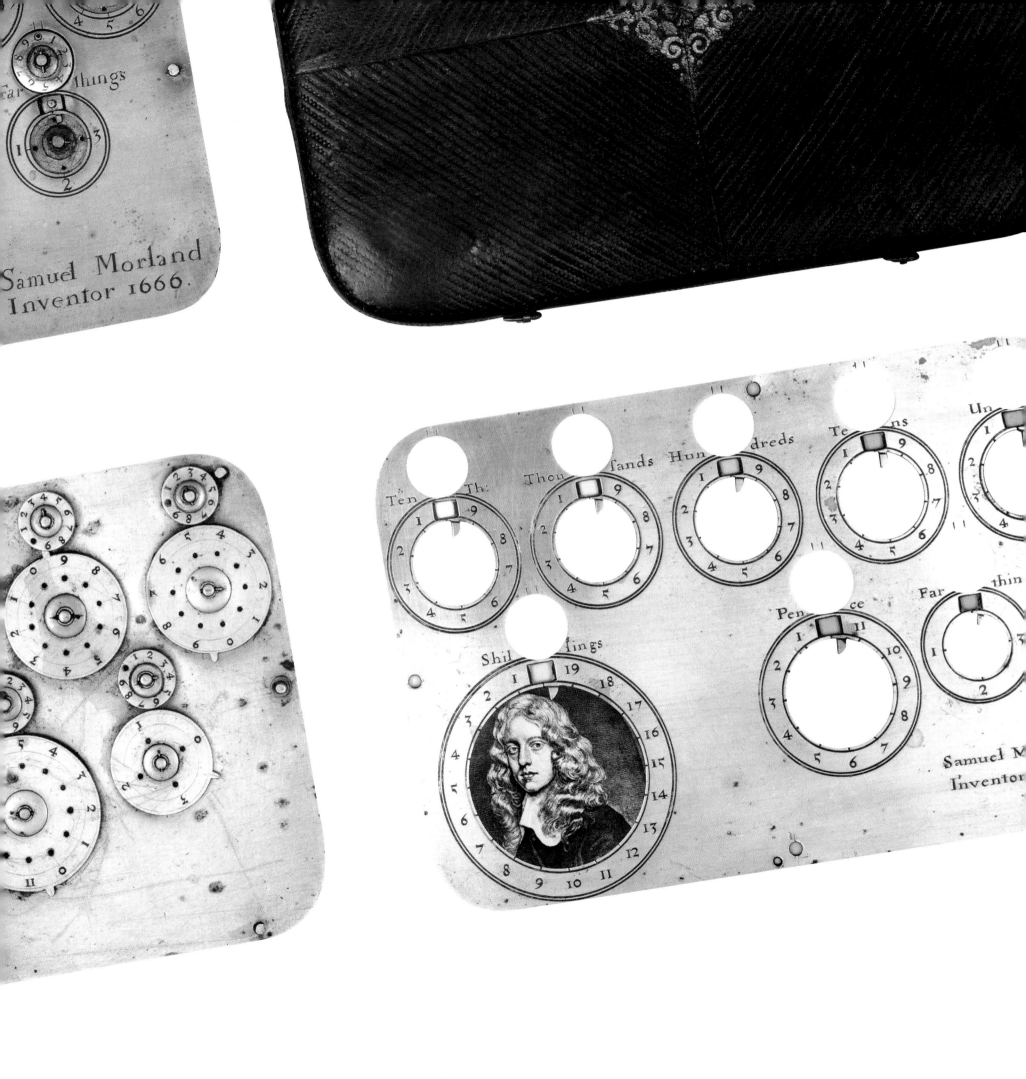

Samuel Morland
Inventor 1666.

Ten Th: Thou fands Hun dreds Te ns Un

Shil lings Pence Far thing

Samuel M
Inventor

⟵| Gottfried Wilhelm von Leibniz

Like other pioneers of the early mechanical calculator, Gottfried Wilhelm von Leibniz (1646–1716) was a polymathic genius. He excelled in philosophy, logic maths, history, law, mechanics and languages. He developed the principles of calculus independently of Sir Isaac Newton and invented the binary number system, which is the foundation of modern computers. He wrote that he had invented his calculator because "it is unworthy of excellent men to lose hours like slaves in the labour of calculation which could safely be regulated to anyone else if machines were used".

↑ Stepped Reckoner

When Leibniz invented his calculator in 1673, he was unaware of the work of Pascal or Schickard. His device, known as the Stepped Reckoner or the Arithmetical Engine, was much more sophisticated than either the Pascaline or the Calculating Clock, in that it could perform all four arithmetical functions. Unfortunately, the manufacturing technology of the late seventeenth century was not good enough to manufacture Leibniz's calculator properly and he was never able to commercialize it. Leibniz spent his later years arguing that he had invented calculus before Newton, and he died poor and friendless.

↓ Large-scale Arithmometer

The Paris Exhibition of 1855 introduced the world to the revolutionary progress that was taking place in machinery, chemistry, lighting, heat, electricity and manufacturing processes. To help prove the point that technology was on the march, the exhibition commissioned the Frenchman Charles Xavier Thomas de Colmar (1785–1870) to build a fancy, large-scale working model of his famous Arithmometer. Using the same mechanism as his famed table-top model, Thomas's gold-encrusted piano-style Arithmometer won the gold medal. With 15 input keys and a 30-digit display, the filigreed behemoth was designed for rapid assembly and disassembly, which made it relatively easy to transport.

↑ Philipp Matthäus Hahn

Philipp Matthäus Hahn (1739–1790) was a mechanical engineer and theologian from Württemberg, Germany. Known for his astronomical clocks, watches and balances, he also designed cylindrical calculating machines based on the Leibniz mechanism. Hahn's design was improved upon by his student, Johann Christoph Schuster (1759–1823), who reduced the size of the components and made it easier to use. Schuster's devices, which he started to make in 1792, represent the last of the pre-Industrial Age calculators.

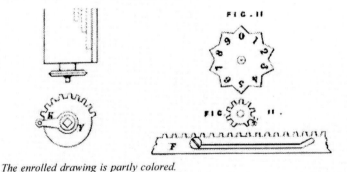

Drawings 1 of Thomas De Colmar's English Patent 13,504 (1851)

FIG. II

FIG. II.

The enrolled drawing is partly colored.

London:Printed by George Edward Eyre and
Printers to the Queen's most Excellen

(*text*)   (*Drawing II*)

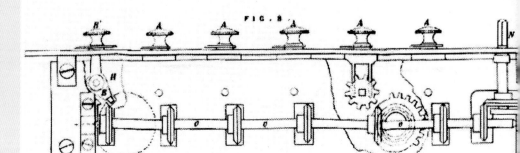

FIG. 8.

eorge Edward Eyre and William Spottiswoode,
Queen's most Excellent Majesty. 1857.

Odhner calculating machine

If you were working in an office as late as 1975, you may have seen an Odhner machine. They were commonplace items in accounting firms throughout the twentieth century, until the advent of the four-function electronic calculator made them obsolete. To add with an Odhner machine, you first entered a number, one digit at a time, by moving a setting lever. Once the number was entered, you turned the crank. Then you entered a second number and turned the crank again. The result was displayed in the product register. Subtraction, multiplication and division all required different input methods.

Willgodt Theophil Odhner

Willgodt Theophil Odhner (1845–1905), a Swedish engineer living in St Petersburg, Russia, built his first calculating machine, with its distinctive hand-crank and cylindrical body, in 1874. Sturdy, compact and reliable, the machine was sold under many names, including Arrow, Brunsviga, Dactyle Britannic, Eclair, Marchant, Rapide, Triumphator and Vaucanson. Known as a pinwheel, or variable cog, or calculator, the Odhner machine contained as many as 700 parts and was made possible only as a result of the advanced level of manufacturing technology of the day.

↑ Comptometer

Self-educated American Dorr E Felt (1862–1930) built his first mechanical calculator in 1884 out of staples, elastic bands, meat skewers and a wooden macaroni box. Felt refined his invention, which was dubbed the Comptometer, and in 1887 the US Treasury bought four of them. When other organizations began buying the keyboard-equipped Comptometers, Felt founded a chain of Comptometer schools around the world to train and deploy "keyboardists" to use the calculating machines. A fast keyboardist could perform as many as 200,000 keystrokes per day. About 20,000 Comptometers were sold during the next 30 years. In 1915 a model was made that offered error detection and correction. It proved immensely popular and 42,000 examples were sold during the next five years. The Felt & Tarrant Manufacturing Company (later called the Comptometer Corporation) continued to make Comptometers into the 1970s.

←| Kelvin's Tide Predictor

Almost every computer in existence is based on digital technology, which means it uses numeric code to perform calculations. But in the early days of computing, some scientists made machines that modelled real-life phenomena by using analogue – or continuously varying – signals. One of the most famous was Kelvin's Tide Predictor of 1876. Lord Kelvin (1824–1907), who was fêted for his work on the first transatlantic cable (which earned him his title), was also a major contributor to the advancement of physics. Extremely gifted and supremely arrogant, Kelvin had his share of successes (many of his 300 papers on physics were of profound importance) and failures (in 1895 he told the Australian Institute of Physics that "heavier-than-air flying machines are impossible"). One of his most impressive achievements was the Tide Predictor, which simulated the gravitational pull of the moon on the Earth by means of a complex arrangement of pulleys, gears, shafts and wires. In this way, it was able accurately to calculate the height and time of high and low tides for any day of the year that the user dialled in.

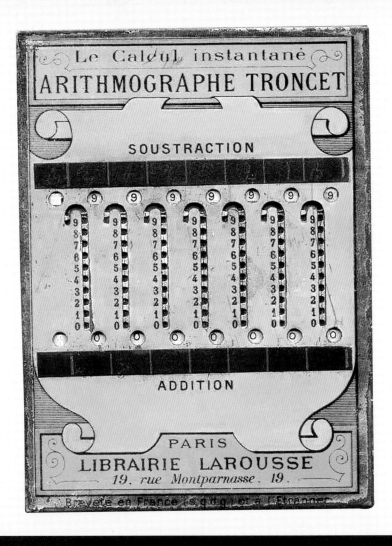

Arithmographe slide adder

By the late nineteenth century, manufacturing technology and mechanical know-how had reached a point where low-cost, miniature calculators were possible. The most famous was the Arithmographe slide adder, invented by Frenchman J-L Troncet in 1888. While he borrowed ideas from earlier calculator inventors, Troncet popularized the concept. The glut of imitations that followed the Arithmographe were often called "troncets". Something like an automated abacus, the Arithmographe contained notched metal strips that could be moved with a stylus. In the 1960s and 1970s, slide adders were sold for a dollar in the back of comic books.

Burroughs adding machine

By 1887 former bank clerk William Seward Burroughs (1857–1898) had made 50 adding machines based on his patent. Unfortunately, he had trouble selling them at US$475 each because he was the only person who could make them work correctly. He went back to the drawing board and came up with an improved model. His company, American Arithmometer, sold 284 in 1895, the same year he founded Burroughs Adding and Registering Company in Nottingham, England. His machine, and the company that made it, became a resounding success that set the stage for large-scale industrial number crunching, but Burroughs didn't survive to enjoy it. He succumbed to chronic health problems at the age of 43. (Ironic, when you consider that his more famous grandson, author William Seward Burroughs, lived to the ripe age of 83 despite decades of reckless drug use.)

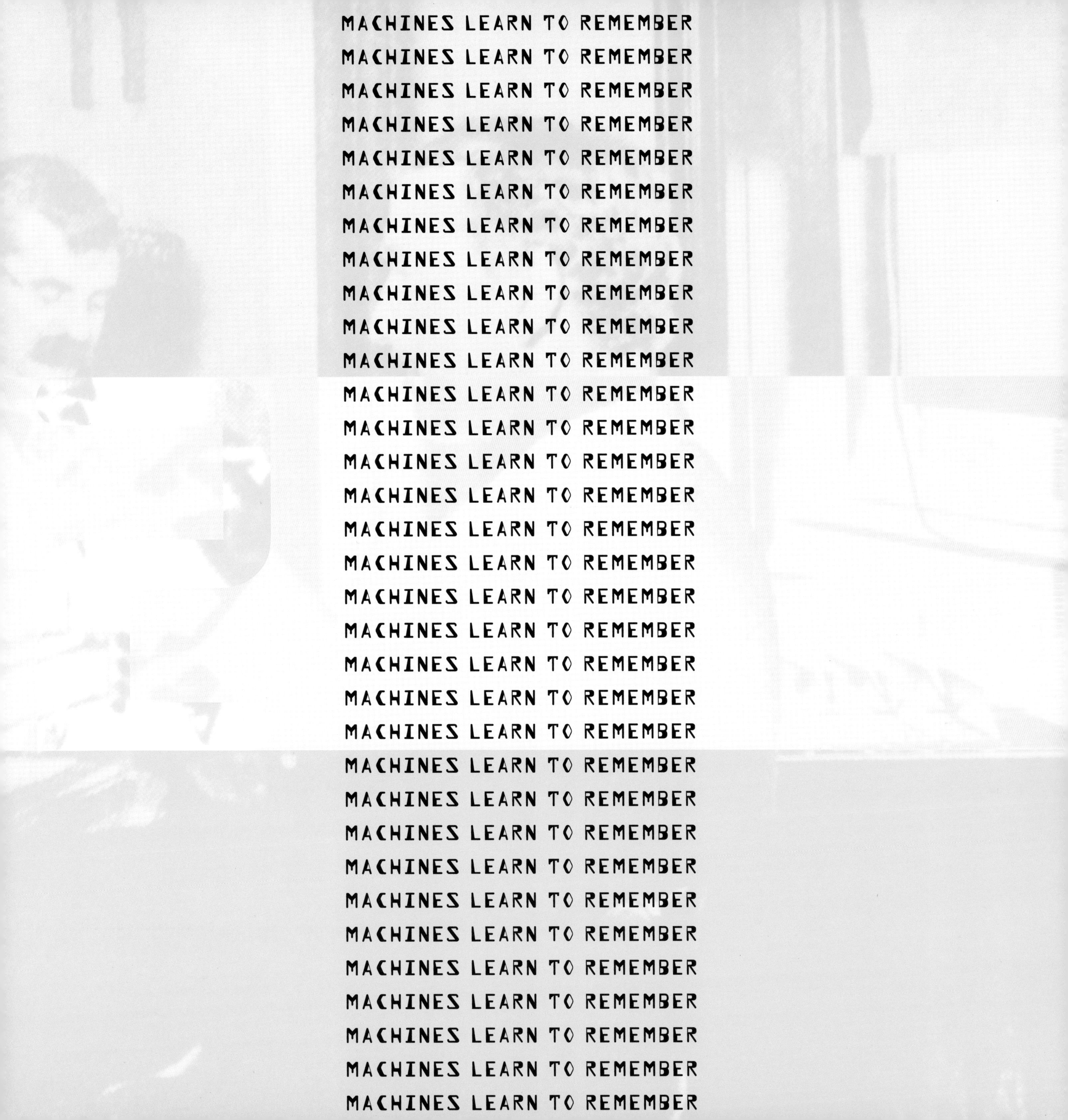

MACHINES LEARN TO REMEMBER

MACHINES LEARN TO REMEMBER

MACHINES LEARN TO REMEMBER

MACHINES LEARN TO REMEMBER

MACHINES LEARN TO REMEMBER

MACHINES LEARN TO REMEMBER

MACHINES LEARN TO REMEMBER

MACHINES LEARN TO REMEMBER

MACHINES LEARN TO REMEMBER

MACHINES LEARN TO REMEMBER

MACHINES LEARN TO REMEMBER

MACHINES LEARN TO REMEMBER

MACHINES LEARN TO REMEMBER

MACHINES LEARN TO REMEMBER

MACHINES LEARN TO REMEMBER

MACHINES LEARN TO REMEMBER

MACHINES LEARN TO REMEMBER

MACHINES LEARN TO REMEMBER

MACHINES LEARN TO REMEMBER

MACHINES LEARN TO REMEMBER

MACHINES LEARN TO REMEMBER

MACHINES LEARN TO REMEMBER

MACHINES LEARN TO REMEMBER

MACHINES LEARN TO REMEMBER

MACHINES LEARN TO REMEMBER

MACHINES LEARN TO REMEMBER

MACHINES LEARN TO REMEMBER

MACHINES LEARN TO REMEMBER

MACHINES LEARN TO REMEMBER

MACHINES LEARN TO REMEMBER

MACHINES LEARN TO REMEMBER

MACHINES LEARN TO REMEMBER

MACHINES LEARN TO REMEMBER

In the late eighteenth century, Britain was the world's most powerful colonial empire. With the goods it imported from its colonies, the vast resources of coal and iron in its home country, and its emphasis on science and exploration, Britain was the birthplace of the Industrial Revolution. Giant, coal-fired steam engines powered the machinery inside factories that employed thousands of former farm workers to manufacture products that had been formerly cobbled, stitched, coopered, smithed and riveted by rural craftspeople using hand tools.

As the new factories produced goods, they also produced numbers, and the need to process numbers. Quotas, yields, orders, projections, payrolls, loans, taxes – suddenly, people were overwhelmed by the need to figure out what had happened, what was happening, and what was going to happen. All this required computers. In those days, a computer wasn't a machine, but a person. Businesses, government bodies and universities hired human computers to generate tables of numbers, which were used for scientific calculations, celestial navigation, insurance calculations and other number-intensive activities.

The human computation process worked like this: several mathematicians would lead a table-making project. They'd develop the specific algorithms (step-by-step instructions that required nothing more than basic arithmetic) to be used to generate the numbers. Then human computers applied algorithms to sets of data and crunched the numbers by hand. Their work was supervised by foremen and rechecked by other computers.

Despite the chain of command, errors were unavoidable. They occurred in the calculating phase and they were also introduced by typesetters who prepared plates for printing. The errors could sometimes have disastrous consequences. In the case of navigational tables for determining longitude at sea, for instance, a mistake could result in great delays, or worse.

One man thought he had the solution. His name was Charles Babbage (1791–1871) and his idea was to take the power of the Industrial Revolution and apply it to solving the problems created by it. He wanted to replace error-prone human computers with infallible steam-powered machines. He thought of the idea for a table-calculating machine in 1812 or 1813, while attending an undergraduate maths club at Cambridge University. He didn't consider it again until 1820 or 1821, when he was checking some tables for the Royal Astronomical Society. After discovering errors, Babbage told his colleague: "I wish to God these calculations had been executed by steam." His colleague encouraged him to develop a steam-powered computer and Babbage set to work designing one. After studying the problem for some months, he wrote a paper entitled *On the Theoretical Principles of the Machinery for Calculating Tables.*

Babbage's design for a machine, which he called the Difference Engine, would not only calculate sets of tables flawlessly, it would also stamp out the plates used to print them, thus eliminating all possibilities for error (save the ones that some publishers purposely introduced in order to catch copyright infringers). That year, he approached the Astronomical Society with his proposal for a 3-ton, 25,000-part Difference Engine and he was awarded grants totalling £17,000 (an enormous sum of money for the time) to develop it. As it turned out, though, no amount of money would have been enough to complete the project. The machine was far too complex to be built and Babbage never got past making partial models of the machine. He dipped deeply into his own £100,000 inheritance, but it turned out that money wasn't the only problem.

Babbage was a difficult person to work with, and his chief engineer, Joseph Clement, was equally stubborn and also fond of inflating his expenses. In 1827, with no end in sight, Babbage experienced a series of tragedies. First his father died, then his second son, followed shortly thereafter by his wife and newborn son. He suffered a breakdown and went to Europe for a year, leaving the project in the hands of Clement, who let it languish.

When Babbage returned to Britain, he resumed work on the engine. By 1832 he had succeeded in building part of the machine and tests showed that it worked exactly as he had hoped. However, by this time Babbage had already conceived of a far more complex machine, which he called the Analytical Engine. Babbage pleaded with the government for funding to build the fantastic new machine, which had many of the same functions of a modern-day computer, including the ability to store programmes in memory. He also adopted the idea of using punch cards (commonly used in automatic weaving looms to produce complex patterns in fabric) to feed data to the engine. But the government was tired of giving money to Babbage without getting results. In 1842 the Prime Minister killed the project and, along with it, Babbage's dreams of a computerized Britain.

Such grand-scale visions wouldn't be seen again for almost half a century, when a young man named Herman Hollerith, an American born to German immigrants, went to work for the US Census Bureau. This time, the vision resulted in astounding success. Hollerith developed a punch-card tabulating system that revolutionized census-taking. To operate the machine, the human operator inserted a card in the reader and pulled a handle. This caused spring-loaded electrical contacts to drop on to the card. Wherever there was a punched hole, the contact above it would go through the hole in the card and touch a small reservoir of mercury, which would complete a circuit that would cause the appropriate dial indicator to advance incrementally. The counting dials had two hands and worked like a clock. The difference was that the dials had 100 positions, not 60. Each time the large hand went all the way around the dial, the smaller hand would advance by one. Thus a dial could count to 9,999 before rolling back to zero.

Babbage's dream of a gleaming brass, steam-powered computer was much grander than Hollerith's tabulators. But Babbage was born too early. Hollerith's tabulating machines soon found use in other industries and his company merged with two other data processing firms. The new company was called the Computer-Tabulating-Recording Company, or C-T-R. In 1924 C-T-R changed its name to International Business Machines, now better known as IBM.

Joseph Marie Jacquard

When Joseph Marie Jacquard's father, a weaver, died, he left two looms for his son. Jacquard attempted to run his own weaving business, but his insatiable desire to tinker with the mechanical processes of the machines drove him to bankruptcy. For a number of years, he worked as a lime burner while his wife wove straw. In his spare time, he continued to work on his loom improvements, and in 1801 he showed his punch-card-controlled loom at an industrial exhibition in Paris. Silk weavers were opposed, sometimes violently, to Jacquard's automated looms, but progress won out: by 1812 more than 11,000 Jacquard Looms were in operation. Napoleon was so impressed by the looms that he awarded Jacquard a pension for life, and a royalty on each machine sold.

Jacquard Loom

The Jacquard Loom is one of the finest examples of industrial age automation. Before Joseph Marie Jacquard's invention was introduced, only very simple patterns could be mass produced by automatic weaving machinery. Complicated patterns had to be performed by highly skilled and expensive silk weavers. Jacquard's labour-saving loom used a loop of punched cards tied together with string. The holes in the cards allowed specific rods to pass through, which created the desired pattern. The loop of cards cycled through the loom, producing a repeating pattern. A single person could operate the machine and produce yards of material in a fraction of the time that it would take a silk weaver to make them. The punched cards themselves were quite valuable, and were sometimes stolen and copied.

Punched-card technology

Frenchman Joseph Marie Jacquard (1752–1834) revolutionized the weaving industry with the invention of his Jacquard Loom. Fabrics with intricate patterns, like the one shown here, could now be woven automatically, thanks to a series of punched cards that stored the patterns and a reader that interpreted the coding on the cards, much in the same way that a pianola produces music stored on rolls of punched paper. Jacquard didn't invent punched cards (that was done by another Frenchman, Jean Falcon, in 1728), but he combined Falcon's idea with another loom innovation, a cylinder mechanism designed by automaton maker Jacques Vaucanson (1709–1782), to come up with his world-changing machine. Both Charles Babbage and Herman Hollerith (founder of the company that became IBM) used punched cards for their own computers.

Charles Babbage

British mathematician and inventor Charles Babbage (1791–1871) was the first person to design a programmable computer and he is considered by most historians to be the father of modern computing. Babbage conceived of his machines as a way to automate the production of reference tables used by insurance actuaries, ships' navigators and engineers. Babbage's machines would not only generate the tables by means of punched-card programmes, they would also produce the plates used to print the tables, thereby eliminating the errors introduced when printers manually set the type for the printing plates. Although his beautiful mechanical computer designs were never built, a working model, accurate to 31 decimal places, was made from his original plans in 1991.

Difference Engine

In 1822 Charles Babbage went to the Royal Society to propose his idea for a Difference Engine to produce navigation and industrial tables. His device would consist of thousands of interlocking gears and would be powered by a steam engine. A year later, he had built a hand-cranked six-digit calculator that employed the basic concepts of a full-sized Difference Engine. In 1823 Babbage received a grant from the British government to proceed with the design and manufacture of the device. Unfortunately for Babbage, though, his idea came about 30 years too soon. The technology to manufacture a device of such precision wouldn't be readily available until 1850 or so. As a result, Babbage quickly ran out of money in his attempt to advance the state of engineering technology. For the next ten years, the government pumped additional funds into the endeavour, totalling £17,000 (and Babbage contributed further thousands from his personal fortune). In 1833 Babbage unveiled a small proof-of-concept prototype, which demonstrated the soundness of the device's principles, but it was too small to perform useful work. It also couldn't print. Today, the prototype, which stands 2 ft (60 cm) tall, is in the Science Museum in London, England, and still in perfect working condition.

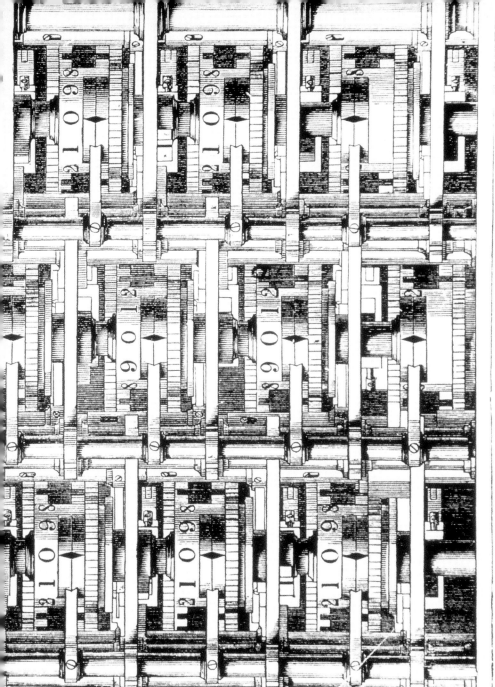

George Boole

Self-educated British mathematician and philosopher George Boole (1815–1864) boiled down logic to a set of symbols when he invented Boolean algebra in 1847. His brilliant work was all but ignored for nearly a century. Today, Boole's logic system is the basis for all digital electronics. The microscopic electronic switches in integrated circuits are Boolean "gates" that produce a specific output for a given input. For example, an OR gate outputs a "zero" when both inputs are "zero", and yields a "one" when either or both inputs are "one". An AND gate outputs a "one" when both inputs are "one", and outputs a "zero" in all other conditions.

Difference Engine #2

Charles Babbage set to work on Difference Engine #2 between 1847 and 1849. Realizing that his first machine was far too complicated, this new machine required only one-third of the number of parts used by the original, yet it was just as powerful. But Babbage was unable to build it. With 4,000 moving parts, it was still too challenging for the tradesmen of the day to make without going to great expense. Historians also believe that Babbage's unpleasant personality and disagreements with his main engineer, Joseph Clement, prevented the machine from being completed.

Ada Byron Lovelace

When Ada Byron Lovelace (1815–1852) was only one month old, her mother left her father, Lord Byron. She was raised by her mother, who was so frightened that she would grow up to be a poet, as her father was, that she schooled her daughter in maths and science. Lovelace met Charles Babbage in 1833 and became fascinated with his machines. In 1842 she translated an Italian mathematician's article about the Analytical Engine into English, and included her own lengthy notes in the article, which was published in a British science journal. In her notes she wrote: "We may say most aptly that the Analytical Engine weaves algebraic patterns just as the Jacquard loom weaves flowers and leaves." As Babbage's biggest champion, she predicted that computers would one day be commonplace in people's houses. Like Pascal, Lovelace was honoured with a computer language named after her – Ada.

↦ **Analytical Engine**

Charles Babbage's greatest achievement was the design for his Analytical Engine, a true general purpose computer that could store programmes in its mechanical memory. Babbage conceived of it in 1837. Powered by a steam engine, it called for a massive brass machine that measured more than 30 yards (27m) long. Complete with a printer, plotter and bell to signal the completion of a task, the Analytical Engine (had it been possible to build it) could have changed the path of world history. Babbage wrote in his autobiography: "As soon as an Analytical Engine exists, it will necessarily guide the future course of the science." He continued to work on the project until his death in 1871. In 1878 the British Association for the Advancement of Science recommended that the project be abandoned.

↦ ↦ **Punched holes from ancient Greece**

The programming language that Charles Babbage developed for the Analytical Engine was similar to the programming languages used today. The machine could store up to 1,000 50-digit numbers – more memory than many of the early personal computers had. Babbage's design called for punched cards. The idea was not new. Punched cards were used in weaving looms and, long before that, by the ancient Greeks, who would punch holes in rectangular bars of clay to keep records.

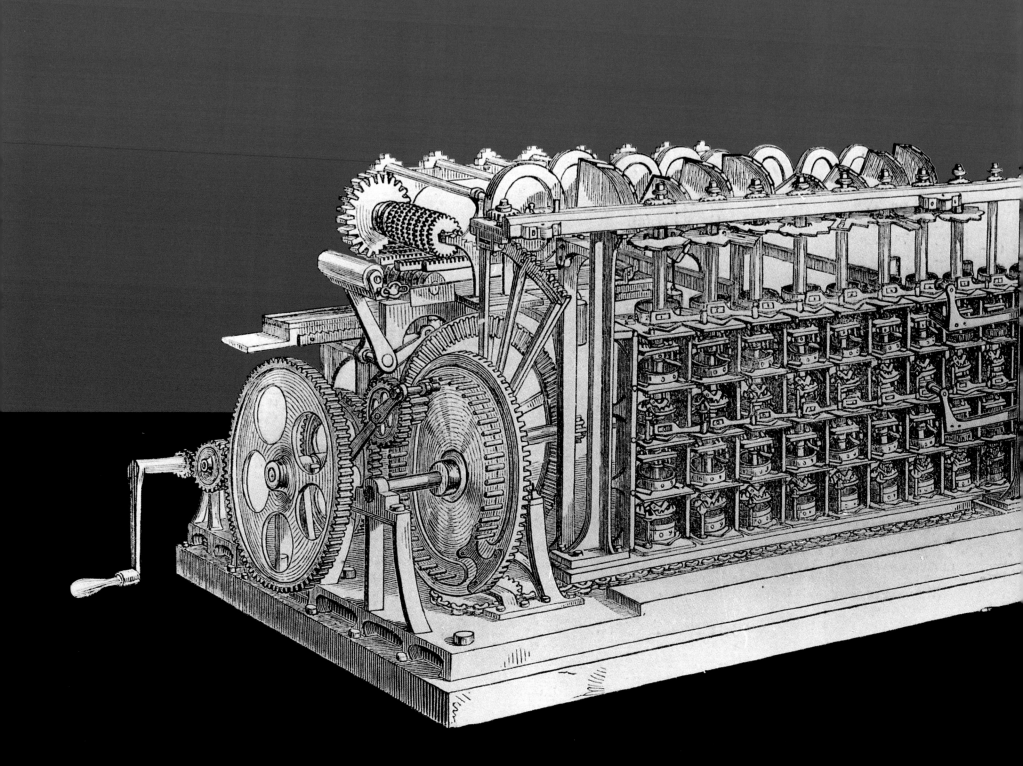

Scheutz's Difference Engine In 1834 George Scheutz, a printer in Stockholm, Sweden,

read an account in the *Edinburgh Review* of Babbage's Difference Engine. From the

limited information provided in the article, Scheutz managed to make a wooden

model. Entranced by the possibilities, he continued to be obsessed by

the Difference Engine and in 1837 he enlisted the help of

his engineer son, Edvard, to build a metal version of the engine.

Completed in 1853, the Scheutz engine won a gold medal at the Great

Exhibition in Paris. Today, it is part of the collection at the

Smithsonian Institution in Washington, DC.

↑ Hollerith Tabulator and Sorter

The Hollerith Tabulator and Sorter was a masterpiece of nineteenth century technology. Housed in a handsome wooden cabinet, the electromechanical data processor accepted punched cards containing statistical data and sorted the cards into pre-specified categories. The cards were then run through a tabulator, which detected the holes and advanced one of the 40 clock-like counters on the front of the machine. The machine was blindingly fast compared to a human, but its cost benefits were questionable. The 1880 census, which used human tabulators, cost US$5.8 million and took nine years to finish. The 1890 census, which used the Hollerith machine, did the job in a bit under seven years, but cost US$11.5 million. Nevertheless, the Hollerith machine was an instant success: Australia, Canada, France, and Russia ordered them for their own censuses.

3

SPARKS OF AN IDEA
SPARKS OF AN IDEA
SPARKS OF AN IDEA
SPARKS OF AN IDEA
SPARKS OF AN IDEA
SPARKS OF AN IDEA
SPARKS OF AN IDEA
SPARKS OF AN IDEA
SPARKS OF AN IDEA
SPARKS OF AN IDEA
SPARKS OF AN IDEA
SPARKS OF AN IDEA
SPARKS OF AN IDEA
SPARKS OF AN IDEA
SPARKS OF AN IDEA
SPARKS OF AN IDEA
SPARKS OF AN IDEA
SPARKS OF AN IDEA
SPARKS OF AN IDEA
SPARKS OF AN IDEA
SPARKS OF AN IDEA
SPARKS OF AN IDEA
SPARKS OF AN IDEA
SPARKS OF AN IDEA
SPARKS OF AN IDEA
SPARKS OF AN IDEA
SPARKS OF AN IDEA
SPARKS OF AN IDEA

The first half of the twentieth century was the era of great electronic and computer pioneers: Lee de Forest, American inventor of the vacuum tube that made electronic computers possible; British scientists W H Eccles and F W Jordan, who helped develop electronic computer memory; German physicist and chemist Walther Bothe, who applied the elegance of Boolean algebra to electron circuitry and thereby laid the foundation for computer logic; American university professor Vannevar Bush, who foresaw a global information system that was remarkably similar to today's World Wide Web; Alan Turing, the brilliant British scientist who conceived of computers as we know them today; Claude Shannon, the American scientist who invented information theory while riding his unicycle and juggling down the corridors at Bell Labs; the German Konrad Zuse, who didn't let a lack of funds stop him from building a true computer from recycled telephone parts in his parent's living room; John Vincent Atanasoff, who won a lengthy court battle to claim the title of inventor of the world's first digital electronic computer; and Howard H Aiken, the Harvard maths professor who built computers while other people just dreamed about them.

George Boole (1815–1864) would never have guessed that he would posthumously become an inspiration for them all. Born in Lincoln, England, in 1815 to a tradesman, Boole was an avid learner. Although poor, his father enjoyed studying maths and taught his son everything he knew. By the time he was eight years old, Boole knew as much about mathematics as his father. At the age of 24, Boole submitted a paper to the *Cambridge Mathematical Journal*. It was published under the title "Researches on the Theory of Analytical Transformations". While he understood many branches of mathematics, it was logic that most interested him. Logic was then considered a branch of philosophy, an idea that Boole agreed with to a certain extent, but he also believed that logic could be understood using mathematics. In 1847 he made his case in a paper entitled "The Mathematical Analysis of Logic". So powerful were his arguments that he was awarded a professorship at Queen's College in Ireland, even though he had never attended university himself. It was during this period that he developed his greatest contribution: the invention of what is now called Boolean algebra. He boiled down logic to binary algebraic symbols: true or false, yes or no, on or off, and 1 or 0.

At the time, nobody cared about Boole's binary algebra. It's likely it would have been forgotten were it not for an American logician named Charles Sanders Pierce, who had taken up an interest in Boole's work and introduced it to the USA 12 years after Boole's death. During the 1880s Pierce started looking into how Boolean algebra could be expressed using electrical switches. Pierce spent the next 20 years studying electricity as a way to transmit information, rather than as a means to convey power. With the help of a student, Allan Marquand, Pierce designed an electric logic circuit; however, this was never built.

In 1936, though, a psychologist named Benjamin Burack from Roosevelt College, Chicago, converted Boole's ideas into electricity. He invented the Syllogism Machine – a battery-powered, suitcase-sized electric logic analyzer. The machine used wooden blocks with symbols printed on them. When the blocks were arranged to formulate different propositions, electrical contacts on the blocks would complete a circuit and the machine would determine whether or not a syllogism was valid. For example, if you arranged the blocks to "tell" the machine "All fish have gills. A trout is a fish", it would validate the statement "A trout has gills". If it was not valid, for example "All fish are trout", it indicated which of the seven types of fallacies the statement contained by means of small light bulbs in the case.

Nothing became of Burack's machine, other than its ending up as an exhibit at the Smithsonian Institution in Washington, DC. But Boole's ideas went a lot further with one of Pierce's students, Claude Shannon, whose PhD thesis at the Massachusetts Institute of Technology (MIT) was on calculating Boolean arithmetic using electric switching circuits. When IBM caught wind of Shannon's groundbreaking paper, it hired Harvard professor Howard Aiken to build a Shannon-inspired electrical calculating machine, called the Mark I. But in 1944, when Aiken finished building the clanking behemoth, the technology (but not Boole's ideas) was already out of date. Electrical switches were being replaced by vacuum tubes.

The idea for using vacuum tubes – which are simply light bulbs with specially shaped metallic components in them to control the flow of electricity – came to the American inventor Lee De Forest after he had read about the work of England's John Ambrose, who used tubes to detect radio signals. In 1942 John Atanasoff, a maths professor at Iowa State College, finished building a computer made out of vacuum tubes, which were much faster than the electrical switches in Aiken's Mark I. With the help of his graduate student Clifford Berry and, with a grant of US$650, he built a prototype that could add and subtract eight-digit numbers. He got the go-ahead to build a full-scale computer. When completed in 1942, the 320 kg (700 lb) machine performed two arithmetical operations per second. The Atanasoff-Berry Computer (ABC) used rotating drums lined with capacitors as memory storage devices. A human operator had to control it at every step of the operation. While Atanasoff was building his computer, a physicist named John Mauchly visited him and learned everything he could about Atanasoff's computer. Mauchly went on to co-invent ENIAC (Electronic Numerical Integrator And Computer) with Presper Eckert at the University of Pennsylvania. Today, most computer history books credit ENIAC as the first digital computer. (Zuse and Atanasoff would disagree.)

These machines couldn't really be called computers, however – at least not in the way we know them today. The first person to envisage, and prove the possibility of, machines that could read programmed instructions for any conceivable task and then execute those instructions was a British scientist named Alan Turing. While Turing, who had developed a code-breaking machine during the Second World War to decrypt German ciphers, had the opportunity to put his theory into practice by building programmable computers, his life was cut short when he committed suicide in 1954. Other giants in the computer field, notably John von Neumann, John Mauchley, and J Presper Eckert, carried on his work. The computer age was in full swing. Would Boole have been surprised? It's anyone's guess.

The information age reaches the office

By the end of the nineteenth century, the information age was chugging along. Large office rooms were filled with workers using typewriters, and mechanical and electromechanical tabulating, sorting and calculating devices were a mainstay in number-intensive industries, such as accounting, engineering, banking, manufacturing and insurance. By 1928 the top five business machine companies had combined revenues of more than US$179 million (about US$1.9 billion in today's money).

Vacuum tube

In 1906 Lee de Forest (1873–1961), an American inventor interested in radio, read about the attempts of Englishman John Ambrose Fleming (1849–1945) to make a radio signal detector using the Edison Effect (in which a current applied to a bulb with a plate in it moves from the filament to the plate). Fleming failed in this effort, but he discovered something more interesting: when radio signals went through the modified bulb, the current from the bulb varied in proportion to the signals. By adding a speaker to the bulb, you could hear the radio waves. De Forest improved Fleming's tube by adding a metallic element between the filament and the plate, which greatly amplified the radio signals it received. He called the tube the Audion and it launched a new era in electronics.

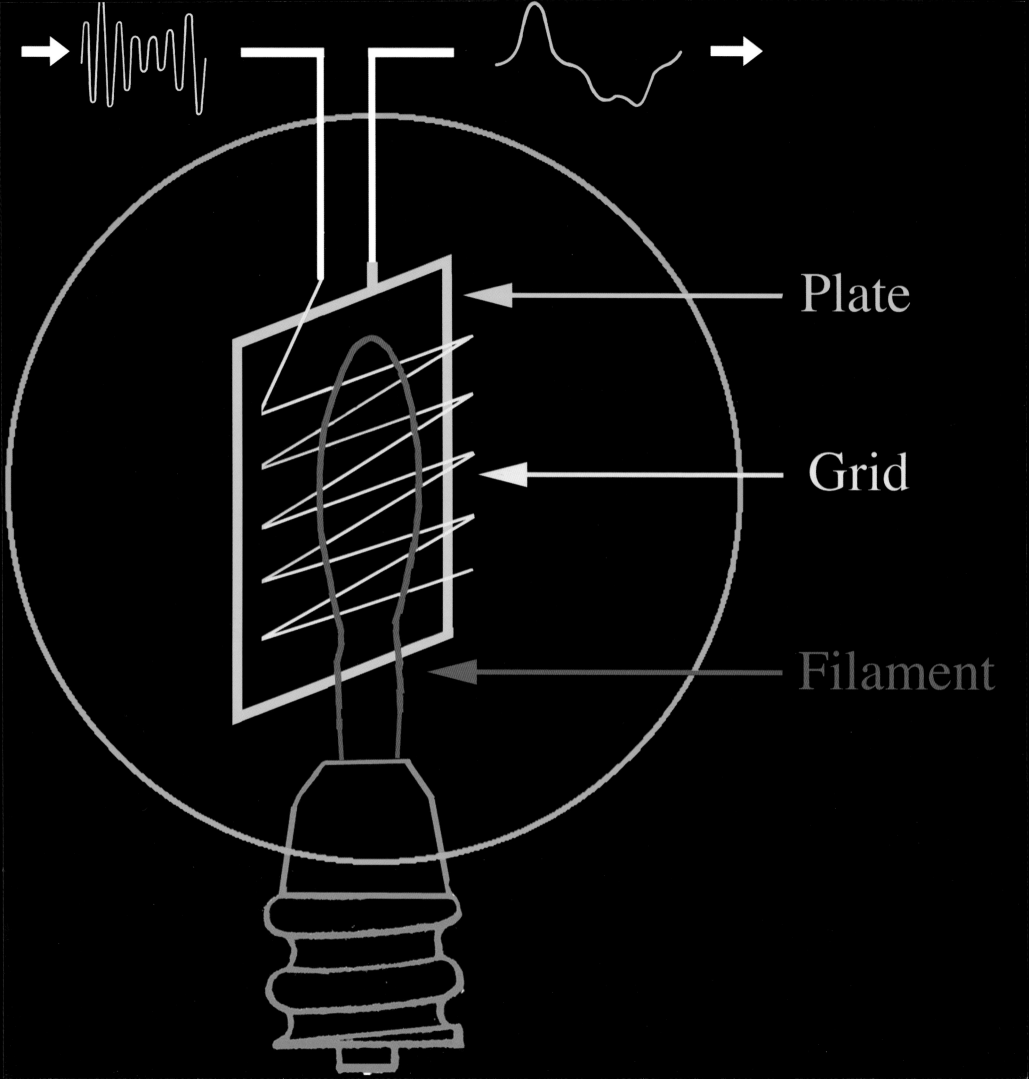

The latch circuit

In 1919 British scientists W H Eccles (shown here) and F W Jordan invented an electronic "bi-stable latch circuit". When an electrical signal was applied to one of its inputs, the electrical state of the output was reversed. This was, in effect, a one-bit memory storage device. Andrew D Booth, a British information technologist, later remarked about the invention: "At any time from that moment on, a modern computer could have been built." In the 1940s the latch circuit came to be known as the flip-flop circuit, because of the way the output signal flips or flops with each pulse it receives. Early computers used two vacuum tubes for each single bit of memory. Compare that to the hundreds of millions of bits of memory contained in a single silicon chip in today's personal computers. Here Eccles is demonstrating another invention: a wireless device that generated vowel sounds on the receiving unit.

Boolean algebra

In 1847 George Boole (1815–1864) invented Boolean algebra, which consisted of logical symbols that could be arranged in "circuits", much like the binary circuitry that appears in computers today. In 1899 electricity pioneer Nikola Tesla patented an electromechanical AND gate, and in 1924 German physicist and chemist Walther Bothe (1891–1957), who is shown here, invented an electronic AND gate, which led the way to digital circuits. An AND gate has two inputs and one output. When both inputs have a current applied to them, the output is "high". If one or both inputs do not have a current applied to it, the output is low. The AND gate is one of seven basic logic gates: AND, OR, XOR (exclusive OR), NOT, NAND (negative AND), NOR (negative OR) and XNOR (exclusive negative OR). It's possible to build a flip-flop circuit – and, indeed, any other digital component – from a combination of different logic gates.

Reynold B Johnson

When Reynold B Johnson (1906–1998) was a boy growing up in Minnesota, he liked to play a trick on his sister's boyfriends. Whenever one of them parked his car at the Johnsons' house, young Reynold would sneak over to the car, open the hood and draw pencil marks on the spark plugs. Graphite is electrically conductive and when the boyfriend tried to start his car, the spark from the spark plug would be attracted to the pencil mark, which prevented the engine from starting. By 1932 Johnson had become a high school teacher. Remembering the pencil prank, he invented a machine that automatically graded his students' multiple-choice tests by detecting the presence of pencil graphite. He went to IBM with his electromechanical contraption but was politely told that they were not interested. A couple of years later, they decided to buy the patent – and hired Johnson as well. He turned out to be a tremendous asset for the company. A veritable invention-making machine, Johnson led the team that invented the first hard disk drive in 1955.

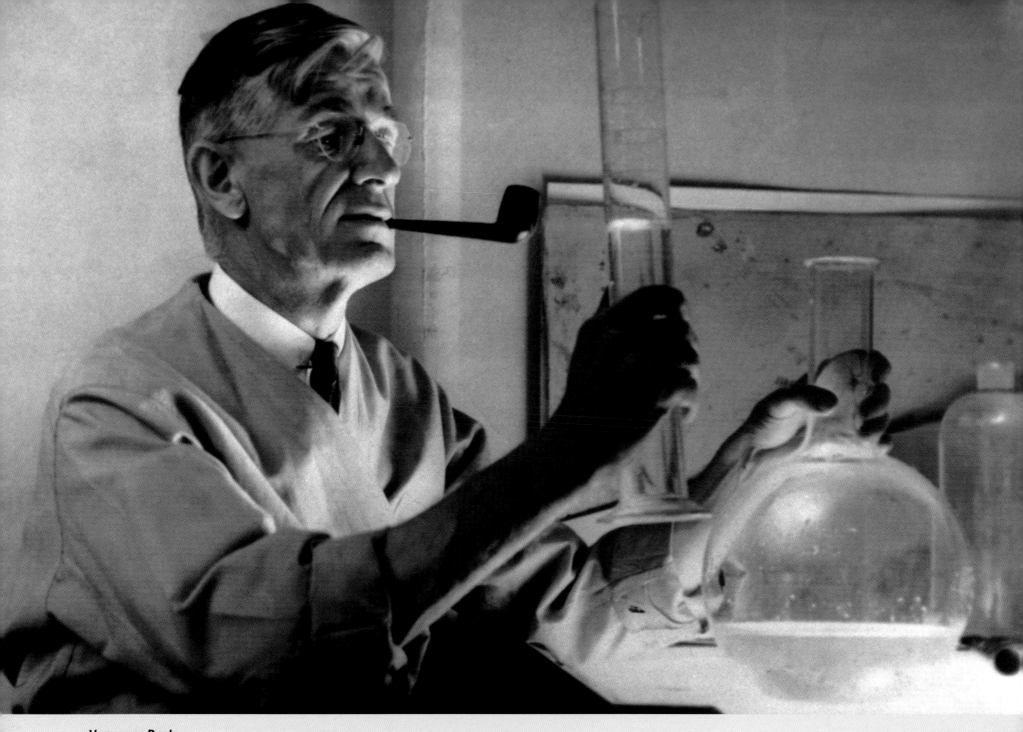

Vannevar Bush

From 1928 to 1932, MIT professor Vannevar Bush (1890–1974) built a "differential analyzer", a gigantic assemblage of rods and gears that solved complex differential equations. In the 1930s he conceived of a microfilm machine that could read 1,000 fingerprints per minute. The FBI declined his proposal, but his idea was the basis for his dream machine, which he called the "memex". In an essay he wrote for the *Atlantic Monthly* in July 1945, entitled "As We May Think", Bush foresaw the development of hypertext and the World Wide Web. He stated: "Wholly new forms of encyclopedias will appear, ready made with a mesh of associative trails running through them, ready to be dropped into the memex and there amplified." Not all of Bush's predictions were so accurate. He also predicted "electronic brains" as large as skyscrapers, whose components would need to be cooled by the equivalent of Niagara Falls.

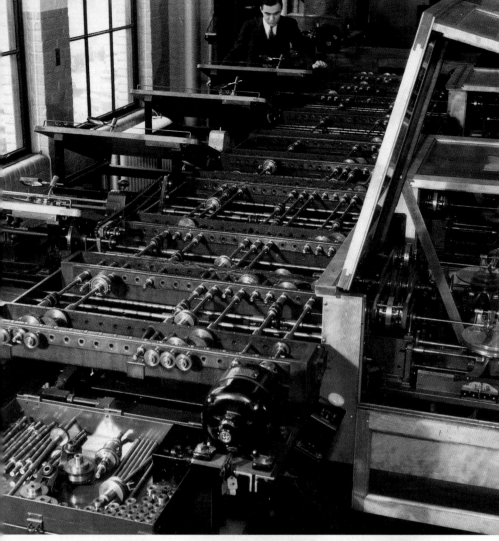

Differential Analyzer

The MIT Differential Analyzer, completed in 1931, used mechanical integrators to solve differential equations, commonly used in engineering. The Differential Analyzer was accurate to within 2 per cent but, like Kelvin's Tide Predictor, it used dead-end analogue technology. Nevertheless, Vannevar Bush was a giant among computer pioneers and he became a trusted science adviser to Franklin Delano Roosevelt during the Second World War. His analyzer was copied around the world and used mainly to generate artillery-firing tables for the military.

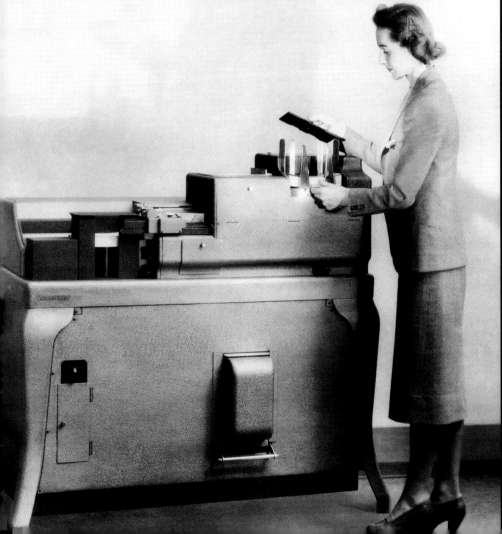

IBM Multiplying Punch

In 1931 IBM introduced the 601 Multiplying Punch, an electrical-relay-based computer. It could read two eight-digit numbers from a card, multiply them and punch the answer back on to a blank part of the card in six seconds. The multiplying punches were a hit in science and industry, and about 1,500 were sold. Later models, including the 602, 603 and 604, were capable of performing additional tasks. From 1948 the 604 was the first of IBM's punches to use vacuum tubes instead of relays and had rudimentary programming capabilities. It was much faster than the 601, as well. It could perform 60 arithmetical operations and punch out the answer in less than one-tenth of a second. Worldwide sales of the 604 reached about 4,000.

Alan Turing

The story of British mathematician Alan M Turing (1912–1954) is
one of the saddest in computer history. A brilliant mathematician and
code breaker, he wrote a paper when he was 25 entitled "On
Computable Numbers, with an Application to the
Entscheidungsproblem" in which he hypothesized a machine that
could solve mathematical problems through the use of a roll of tape
and a scanner-printer that could read and write markings on the
tape. The paper is considered by many to be the beginning of
computer science. He also came up with the Turing Test, which
practically launched the field of Artificial Intelligence. In the Second
World War, he was one of the central figures who broke the German
military's secret code, Enigma. Despite his monumental contributions
to both the war effort and computer science, he was charged with
"gross indecency and sexual perversion" in 1952, when it was
discovered that he was homosexual. He chose to undergo "hormonal
treatment" instead of prison. In 1954 he committed suicide by
eating an apple laced with cyanide.

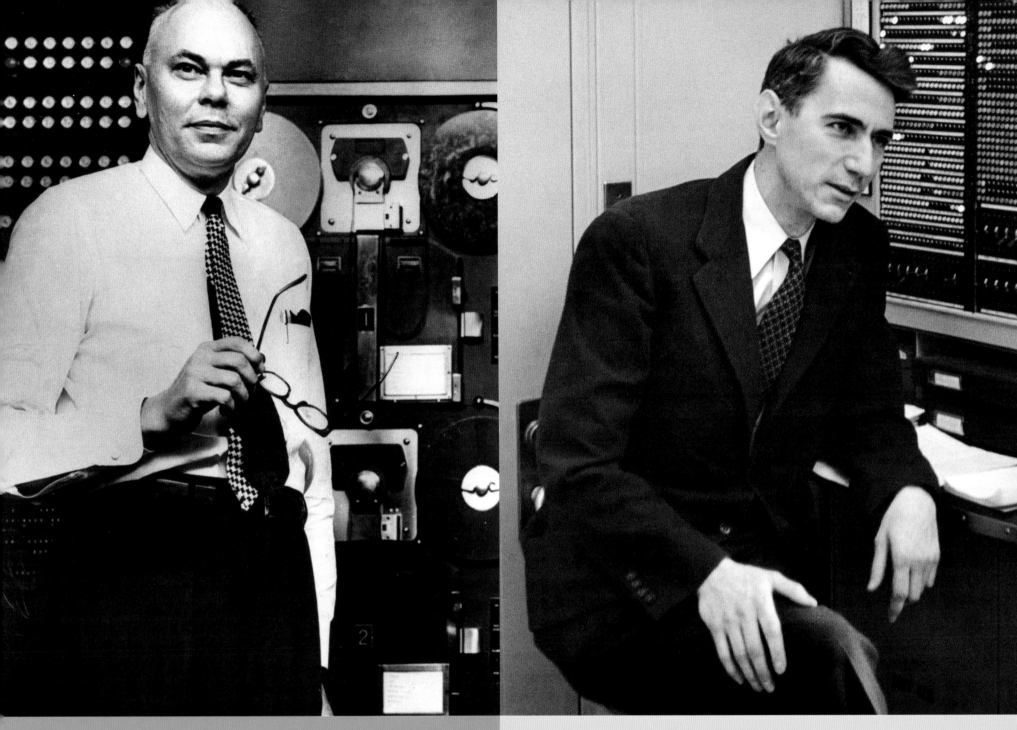

Howard H Aiken

Also in 1937, Howard H Aiken (1900–1973), a Harvard maths professor, came up with the idea for a digital computer that could solve differential equations. After being turned down by a calculator company, he persuaded IBM to back the project, which IBM called the Automatic Sequence Controlled Calculator (and which everyone else called the Harvard Mark I). When it was completed in 1943, the Mark I had three-quarters of a million components, was more than 15m (50 feet) long and weighed 5 tons. When the physicist Jeremy Bernstein visited the room that held the electromechanical behemoth, he later remarked that it made the noise of "a roomful of ladies knitting". Unlike many computer pioneers who carefully guarded their inventions, Aiken had a less secretive outlook. He once said: "Don't worry about people stealing an idea. If it's original, you'll have to ram it down their throats."

Claude Shannon

When Claude Shannon (1916–2001) entered the Massachusetts Institute of Technology in 1936, his professor, Vannevar Bush, put him to work maintaining the gargantuan Differential Analyzer. Shannon soon came to the conclusion that a digital calculator might be better suited for solving complex problems and he wrote his thesis on using Boolean algebra to design electrical circuits. While working at Bell Labs, Shannon single-handedly invented the field of information theory when he published "A Mathematical Theory of Communication" in 1948. He enjoyed juggling while riding his unicycle down the corridors at work and was an inveterate tinkerer, building machines that played chess and solved mazes.

Konrad Zuse's Z1

In 1934 Konrad Zuse (1910–1995) was a statistician at an aircraft company in Dessau, Germany. He became interested in using machines to solve tedious problems, so he gave up his job and started building a mechanical computer in his parents' living room. Completed in 1938, the Z1, as it came to be known, was fully binary and used punched tape to load programmes into the computer's memory. Although the design was theoretically sound, it failed to work because the parts were not manufactured with the necessary precision. The Z1 was destroyed during the Second World War along with the blueprints, but in 1987 Siemens AG and five other companies gave Zuse 800,000 DM to reconstruct the Z1. Then 77 years old, Zuse redrew the plans for the 30,000 parts and rebuilt it in his atelier in Hünfeld between 1987 and 1989. He was held up for six months after a heart attack in 1987 but went on to finish building it with the help of three other people.

George Stibitz's Model K

In 1937 George Stibitz (1904–1995), an American Bell Labs engineer, brought home some flashlight bulbs, spare relays and pieces of a tin tobacco can as part of a self-described "fun project" to build a simple Boolean logic-based binary adder. He dubbed the result the Model K because he put it together on his kitchen table. The adder couldn't do anything more than add two binary numbers together (that is, zeros and ones) and display the result on a pair of light bulbs, but it marked the beginning of electronic digital computing. He later said of the project: "I did not know I was picking up where Charles Babbage in England had to quit over a hundred years before. Nor did it occur to me that my work would turn out to be part of the beginning of what we now know as the computer age." In January 1940 he and a colleague finished what they called the Complex Calculator. Built from 400 telephone relays, the machine accepted input from one of three different teletypes located around Bell Labs Manhattan offices. In late 1940 he connected a fourth teletype located in New Hampshire (250 miles away), making it the earliest example of remote computing.

Differential Analyzer

The MIT Rockefeller Differential Analyzer was
designed by Vannevar Bush and built in 1942. It had
2,000 vacuum tubes, 150 motors and weighed 100
tons. MIT's dean of electrical engineering enthused
that the machine would "mark the beginning of a new
era in mechanized calculus". But it was an analogue
computer, and therefore a dead-end dinosaur. Within
five years the machine – a direct descendant of the
gears-rods-and-levers machines of Leibniz, Babbage
and Kelvin – would be made obsolete by electronic
digital computers.

COMPUTERS GO TO WAR
COMPUTERS GO TO WAR
COMPUTERS GO TO WAR
COMPUTERS GO TO WAR
COMPUTERS GO TO WAR
COMPUTERS GO TO WAR
COMPUTERS GO TO WAR
COMPUTERS GO TO WAR
COMPUTERS GO TO WAR
COMPUTERS GO TO WAR
COMPUTERS GO TO WAR
COMPUTERS GO TO WAR
COMPUTERS GO TO WAR
COMPUTERS GO TO WAR
COMPUTERS GO TO WAR
COMPUTERS GO TO WAR
COMPUTERS GO TO WAR
COMPUTERS GO TO WAR
COMPUTERS GO TO WAR
COMPUTERS GO TO WAR
COMPUTERS GO TO WAR
COMPUTERS GO TO WAR
COMPUTERS GO TO WAR
COMPUTERS GO TO WAR
COMPUTERS GO TO WAR
COMPUTERS GO TO WAR
COMPUTERS GO TO WAR
COMPUTERS GO TO WAR
COMPUTERS GO TO WAR
COMPUTERS GO TO WAR
COMPUTERS GO TO WAR

The Second World War was the first high-technology war. Governments poured millions of dollars into developing calculating machines to do everything from calculate artillery firing tables to crack coded messages. The story really begins in 1918, though, when a German engineer named Arthur Scherbius went to the offices of a company called Gewerkschaft Securitas and showed the owners a device that looked like a portable typewriter. He had purchased the patent from a Dutch designer named Jugo Koch.

It was an electrical cipher machine that could scramble messages by means of three specially constructed rotors that spun around with each press of a key. The company bought Scherbius's patents and, in 1923, went around to trade shows in the hopes of finding buyers for the machine among the post office and other businesses that needed to send secure messages.

Gewerkschaft Securitas didn't drum up much interest among businesses, but the German military started buying the devices, known as "Enigma machines", in 1925. The military added a fourth rotor to the Enigma, giving it the ability to generate scrambled messages in more than 100 sextillion permutations. They also added components to the Enigma that gave it the capability to transmit the messages wirelessly.

Between 30,000 and 100,000 Enigma machines were produced. When a message was created using an Enigma machine, the recipient had to use another Enigma machine set to the same alphabet key to decrypt the message. The keys were changed on a frequent basis (sometimes more than once a day) and delivered by courier to military centres that had Enigma machines. Even if a key was intercepted by the enemy, it would be useless in decrypting any other messages generated using a different key.

The Germans were careful not to let an Enigma machine fall into the wrong hands, because they were afraid that someone could reverse-engineer it and come up with a way to defeat the encryption. But they weren't careful enough. In 1928 the Polish secret service managed to grab one as it passed through customs on its way to the German embassy in Warsaw. The cipher bureau of Poland (the Biuro Szyfrow) went to work on the Enigma, aided in part by documents given to them by a German cipher clerk (who was later executed by the Germans for treason).

The Biuro Szyfrow examined the machine's internal workings. They discovered that the Enigma machine never encoded a letter as itself — in other words, if you typed "D" on the machine, it would never encode it as a "D." This was a serious shortcoming and the Biuro Szyfrow were able to exploit this weakness to crack the codes.

But the Germans kept one step ahead by redesigning the Enigma and making it harder to crack. This time, they used five rotors. After years of unsuccessful attempts to decode scrambled messages from the improved Enigma, the Biuro Szyfrow handed over their findings to the Government Code and Cipher School at Bletchley Park in Buckinghamshire, England. It was here that Allied cryptanalysts cracked the Enigma, first by hand and later by using an electromechanical device called a "bombe", designed by a mathematical genius named Alan Turing. The bombe was able to unscramble messages using "cribbing" – a technique that presumes that a message contains text that can be guessed at. The bombe's rotors spun so quickly that every possible key combination could be tested in just six hours.

While this was going on, a self-trained German computer scientist named Konrad Zuse, cut off from the rest of the world, was trying to convince the Nazis to let him build a computer that would crack the Allied Forces' encoded messages, but he was turned down.

In 1940 178 messages were unscrambled on two Turing bombes. The government quickly ordered more bombes to be made, and by 1945 there were 211 bombes, requiring close to 2,000 people to operate them. The Germans countered by using a new machine, called the Geheimschreiber, which had 10 rotors. The manufacturer, Siemens, was confident that the bombes would never be able to unscramble Geheimschreiber messages – and they were right. The bombes' rotors could spin for centuries and never go through all the different key combinations that the Geheimschreiber was capable of generating.

Not to be defeated, the British developed a fully electronic machine, called the Colossus, that incorporated Turing's theories of statistical code breaking. It was able to emulate a Geheimschreiber and unscramble most messages thrown at it. In all, the British used Turing's bombes and Colossus machines to unscramble nearly 80,000 messages – including crucial communications during the Normandy invasion in 1944. It's no exaggeration to say that Turing made an immense contribution to the Allied victory.

After the war, Turing continued to develop computers. Unlike other computer scientists of the day, he was not just a developer of theories about computers, he was also an excellent engineer who could put his theory into practice. At the National Physical Laboratory, he designed the ACE (Automatic Computing Engine), a fully electronic computer (which wasn't actually built until 1950, after he'd left). In 1949 Turing joined the computing laboratory at the University of Manchester, where he developed software for the Manchester Mark I. In the early 1950s he turned his attention to the mathematics of plant biology, but his work was cut short when he was charged with "gross indecency and sexual perversion" after police reported that he was having a sexual relationship with another man. He was found guilty and lost his security clearance. He never recovered from the setback. Two years later, he died, after eating an apple that had been treated with cyanide.

Today, Turing is getting the respect he deserves. A statue of Turing was erected in Sackville Park, Manchester, in 2001, and another was unveiled at Surrey University in 2004.

⊢→ Electric target computers

Computation has always been an essential element of warfare, from calculating the angle of a trebuchet to controlling unmanned aerial vehicles. In the First World War armies used electric target computers to track moving targets. This computer, from 1922, was used by the US War Department to control heavy artillery.

⊣ Colossus

In 1943, under the code name "Ultra", a team of scientists, headed by M H A Newman and T H Flowers at the British Code and Cipher School at Bletchley Park, built a machine to crack the encoded messages generated by Enigma. Ten machines were built and used. Called the Colossus, the vacuum-tube calculators could process 5,000 characters per second and were used to decode more than 75,000 secret messages. The British government was very careful not to reveal the existence of the Colossus. In fact, there is evidence that Winston Churchill allowed some Nazi bombing raids to occur in England, even though he had advance warning, because he believed that ordering an evacuation or trying to intercept the raid would give away the fact that the British could decode some of the Germans' messages.

⊢→ Enigma

During the Second World War, Nazi Germany transmitted secret messages using the Enigma machine, which had been invented before the war started. After an operator entered a special cipher key (which changed daily, or even more frequently, and was delivered to all Enigma users by courier) into the machine, he would begin typing the message. The electromechanical Enigma would substitute a new letter for each character typed into it, and a new substitution system would come into play with each keystroke. The coded message was then sent by radio to another Enigma operator, who would decode the message using the same cipher key. The British were able to receive the encoded radio signals and even had a stolen Enigma machine in their possession, but without knowing the cipher keys, they were unable to decode the messages.

ENIAC

ENIAC (Electronic Numerical Integrator And Computer) may
not have been the first computer, but it is certainly the most
famous early computer – and for good reason. In 1943
J Presper Eckert and John William Mauchly of the University
of Pennsylvania were commissioned by the US Army's
Ballistics Research Laboratory to design and make a
computer that could generate artillery tables. When the
finished machine was shipped to the Aberdeen Proving
Grounds, Maryland, in 1947, eight women were employed
to programme it by physically rewiring the thousands of
wired connections. The sheer magnitude of ENIAC was
mind-boggling. It had 17,468 vacuum tubes, 7,200 diodes,
1,500 relays, 70,000 resistors, 10,000 capacitors and
nearly five million soldered connections. Because it had so
many tubes, at least a few burned out every day, which made
the machine unusable much of the time. On 2 October 1955
the machine was shut down for good. By then, ENIAC was a
dinosaur among faster, smaller digital beasts.

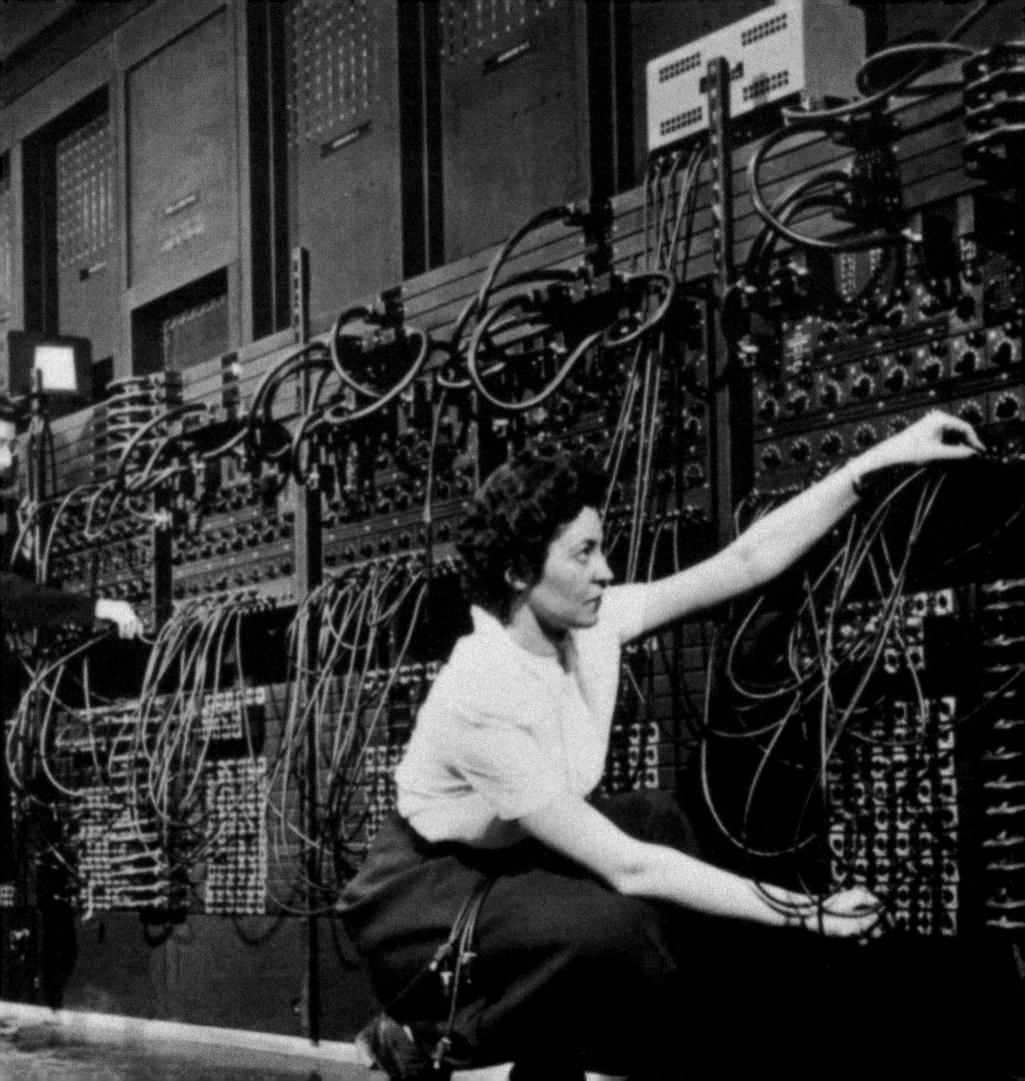

⟵⏐ ↓ ZUSE Z3

Konrad Zuse's Z3 was one of the first programmable computers in the world. Built with recycled materials in 1941 (well before the Colossus in Britain or the ENIAC in the USA) the Z3 had all the components found in a modern computer, except for enough memory to store both a programme and the data. Because Germany was experiencing a paper shortage during the war, the Z3 used discarded movie film as punch tape for storage. Zuse is also credited with developing the first algorithm-based programming language, which he called Plankalkül. The Z3 and all photographs of it were destroyed during an air raid, but Zuse built a working replica in 1960 to protect his patents.

⟵⏐ The expensive "ENY"

ENIAC may have been slow by today's standards, but compared to other mechanical computers at the time, it performed between 100 and 1,000 times faster. Nicknamed "Eny", the room-sized computer cost $500,000 to make (twice the budgeted amount) and wasn't finished in time to do much good during the Second World War. It was used, however, to help design the hydrogen bomb, before it was finally shut down for good at 11:45 pm, 2 October 1955. To commemorate the fiftieth anniversary of ENIAC in 1997, a group of students at Penn State University's Department of Electrical Engineering built a replica of ENIAC on a silicon chip measuring 7.44 mm by 5.29 mm, which held more than 174,000 transistors.

↓ Harvard Mark I

Howard Aiken's Harvard Mark I wins the award for the world's biggest electromechanical calculator. It weighed 5 tons and measured 15.25m by 2.44m (50 ft by 8 ft). The Harvard Mark I, also known as the IBM Automatic Sequence Controlled Calculator, was completed in early 1944 at a cost of US$300,000. Like the other clanking and buzzing behemoths of the era, the Mark I was used to calculate military tables. With 765,000 parts and more than 800km (500 miles) of wire, the Mark I ran for 15 years.

↓ John von Neumann

John von Neumann (1903–1957), standing below right, was one of the mathematical giants of the twentieth century. He could calculate complex maths problems in his head faster than his colleagues armed with a pencil and paper could. During the Second World War, John von Neumann published *First Draft of a Report on the EDVAC*, a groundbreaking document that influenced the development of stored-programme computers (the kind we use today). Such computers are commonly called von Neumann machines in computer science circles, but many other computer pioneers, including Konrad Zuse, Eckert and Mauchly, claim to have conceived of and built stored-programme computers before von Neumann. Here von Neumann is seen with J Robert Oppenheimer. Both men helped lead the Manhattan Project to develop and test the atom bomb.

←┤ The first real computer bug

In the early 1940s the computer researchers at Harvard were calling troublesome computer glitches "bugs". In 1945 Grace Murray Hopper discovered a real bug in the ENIAC. It was a moth that had flown through an open window and landed in a relay, ending its life and shutting down the entire system. Hopper dutifully "debugged" the ENIAC and taped it into her notebook, writing "the first actual case of bug being found". The notebook now resides in the Smithsonian National Museum of American History.

├→ Grace Murray Hopper

In the early days of computing, most of the work was performed by men, but Grace Murray Hopper (1906–1992), one of the first programmers for the Harvard Mark I, was an exception to the rule. She was also the first woman to graduate with a PhD in mathematics from Yale University, in 1934. She joined the Naval Reserve in 1943 and was commissioned as a Lieutenant (Junior Grade). She spent the next four decades as a computer programming language pioneer. Hopper's claim to fame was the invention of the compiler, which is software that takes a programme written by a programmer and converts (compiles) it into the binary code that a computer executes.

DSIR ACE PILOT MODEL 1950

IBM Selective Sequence Electronic Calculator

Occupying nearly half an American football field of floor, the IBM Selective Sequence Electronic Calculator (SSEC) was developed in 1946–1947 by Columbia professor Wallace Eckert (1902–1971), no relation to J Presper Eckert) and a team from the Watson Scientific Computing Laboratory in New York City. Instead of using punched cards, it used huge rolls of uncut punched card stock, each weighing 180 kg (400 lb). With 21,400 relays and 12,500 vacuum tubes, the computer performed its first task, which was to calculate the moon's position, on 27 January 1948. This data was used in the first manned moon mission. In 1952 the SSEC was replaced with IBM's 701, one of the first mass-produced computers.

Automatic Computing Engine

Alan Turing (1912–1954) is notable not only for his uncontested genius in computer theory, but also for his ability to put that theory into practice. He was as interested in relays and vacuum tubes as he was in theorems and principles. In 1945 Turing designed the Automatic Computing Engine (ACE). In 1946 the National Physical Laboratory approved the project, but it wasn't until the May of 1950 that the ACE was completed. It was the first fully electronic computer in London, and the fastest computer in the world, with a clock speed of one Megahertz. (The notebook computer that I used to write this book has a clock speed of 1500 Megahertz.) The architecture of the ACE was used in the Bendix G15 computer. More than 400 were sold and it remained in production until 1970. The British Cold War military computer MOSAIC was also based on the ACE design.

Ferranti Mark 1

Ferranti, a weapons and electronics company, was commissioned by the British government to manufacture this computer. It was based on a prototype known as the Manchester Mark I, which was built at Manchester University in 1946 under the supervision of Professor Max Newman, and for which Alan Turing later built software. Alan Turing had previously been involved with the construction of the ACE (Automatic Computing Engine) at the National Physical Laboratory, and with the construction of "Colossus", the world's first electronic programmable computer, built at Bletchley Park, in Buckinghamshire, during the Second World War.

Satellite tracking

In the 1960s military computers went into orbit. The Cold War-fuelled space race created a need to track the increasing number of artificial satellites circling the planet. Here, deep under Cheyenne Mountain in Colorado Springs, Colorado, the North American Air Defense (NORAD) Command's Battle Staff monitors the orbital path of an American weather-reconnaissance satellite.

5

GETTING DOWN TO BUSINESS
GETTING DOWN TO BUSINESS
GETTING DOWN TO BUSINESS
GETTING DOWN TO BUSINESS
GETTING DOWN TO BUSINESS
GETTING DOWN TO BUSINESS
GETTING DOWN TO BUSINESS
GETTING DOWN TO BUSINESS
GETTING DOWN TO BUSINESS
GETTING DOWN TO BUSINESS
GETTING DOWN TO BUSINESS
GETTING DOWN TO BUSINESS
GETTING DOWN TO BUSINESS
GETTING DOWN TO BUSINESS
GETTING DOWN TO BUSINESS
GETTING DOWN TO BUSINESS
GETTING DOWN TO BUSINESS
GETTING DOWN TO BUSINESS
GETTING DOWN TO BUSINESS
GETTING DOWN TO BUSINESS
GETTING DOWN TO BUSINESS
GETTING DOWN TO BUSINESS
GETTING DOWN TO BUSINESS
GETTING DOWN TO BUSINESS
GETTING DOWN TO BUSINESS
GETTING DOWN TO BUSINESS
GETTING DOWN TO BUSINESS
GETTING DOWN TO BUSINESS
GETTING DOWN TO BUSINESS
GETTING DOWN TO BUSINESS

As a result of the tremendous boost the Second World War had provided to the advancement of computers, a number of companies began adapting wartime technology for peacetime use. Leading the pack was International Business Machines, better known as IBM. Although its roots date back to 1888, the birth of IBM as we know it today really started with the development of the Harvard Mark I computer, designed by Howard Aiken and built in 1943. IBM funded the development of this 5-ton monster, which used electromechanical switches. The loudly clanking machine was so ugly that IBM chairman Thomas Watson ordered it to be covered in a streamlined modern shell to make it look less like an industrial age factory machine and more like a system of the future. The trick worked. The Mark I appeared in the major magazines of the day and IBM became synonymous with electrical efficiency and automation.

Oddly enough, the man who made IBM one of the largest, most successful and most recognized corporations in the world was hesitant to move IBM into the computer business. Thomas J Watson (1874–1956) was born in Campbell, New York, and grew up in a nearby village called Painted Post. After graduating from high school in 1892, Watson found a job as a bookkeeper, for US$6 a week, at Clarence Risley's Meat Market. When a piano and sewing machine salesman offered him twice the income to go and work for him, Watson jumped at the opportunity. But Watson wasn't long for Painted Post. That year he met a flamboyant travelling salesman who promised to teach him the ropes. Watson left with him and soon the pair were selling bank-issued bonds. When the salesman skipped out of town with the proceeds, the bank decided that Watson was guilty by association and fired him.

Broke, Watson found work with National Cash Register (NCR), a successful business machine company run by one of the most colourful characters in American business, John H Patterson. Patterson was a physical fitness nut and made his senior executives join him for 6 am exercise sessions. His sales team – mainly young, white Protestant men – were forbidden from drinking and smoking. They were also required to be scrupulously honest with customers. These strict rules paid off. In 1900 NCR had 2,500 employees and sold 25,000 cash registers per year. By 1910 it was selling 100,000 per year.

In return for conforming to Patterson's rules, NCR employees enjoyed paid vacations, cash bonuses and offices with showers, cafeterias, gymnasiums and doctors' clinics. Watson paid careful attention to the way Patterson ran NCR, and Patterson paid careful attention to Watson. He quickly rose through the ranks and became a trusted executive. Patterson hired him to oversee a campaign to drive dealers of second-hand NCR cash registers out of business. Watson did this by setting up used cash register shops and running a variety of ruses, such as underselling legitimate dealers and selling intentionally faulty machines. Several years later, Patterson, Watson and a couple of dozen other NCR executives were indicted on federal charges for violating anti-trust laws. They were found guilty and Watson was sentenced to a year in prison. He never had to serve the sentence, though, because the public remembered Watson and Patterson for helping the town of Dayton, Ohio, during the floods of 1913.

A year later, Watson was fired on a whim by the capricious Patterson. He got a job at the Computer-Tabulating-Recording Company (C-T-R), which was a merger of four different companies, including the tabulating company Herman Hollerith founded in 1888. As general manager of C-T-R, Watson applied all the good lessons he had learned from NCR, such as excellent conditions and benefits for employees, and only some of the bad ones, like keeping non-whites and non-Protestants off the sales force. He also brought with him NCR's credo, "THINK", which has since become famously associated with IBM.

With Watson at the helm, C-T-R flourished. He kept the company cash-rich by leasing equipment, instead of selling it. The 1920s were good for C-T-R. Its revenues doubled, from US$10 million to US$20 million during that decade. In 1924 Watson changed the company's name to International Business Machines. Even the 1930s was a banner decade for IBM. Businesses had to lay off workers in the Great Depression, but they ended up leasing tabulating machines to replace them. Again, IBM's sales doubled. And when the Second World War broke out, IBM got plenty of business from the military.

Until this point, Watson had avoided building computers. For one thing, there weren't any real computers, aside from a few university lab machines, and Watson didn't see the point in making them when IBM's customers weren't asking for them. He was willing to bankroll the development of computers at universities, however, mainly for the publicity. In 1939 IBM funded the development of Howard Aiken's Harvard Mark I. Although it had cost $500,000 to develop, the Mark I was a tremendous publicity coup for IBM. Encouraged, IBM funded the development of another university computer: Wallace Eckert's Selective Sequence Electronic Calculator (SSEC) for Columbia University. Launched in 1948, the 12,500-tube SSEC was an even bigger hit than the Mark I. IBM installed it next to a ground-level window in its New York offices so people in the street could gawk at the blinking, humming behemoth.

By this time, Watson was well into his seventies and had taken on the role of an elder statesman. His son, Tom, however, was developing new machines that would finally move IBM into the computing business. As early as 1946, Watson Jr was heading up research into electronic calculators, and when IBM offered its first tube-based multiplier, the IBM 603, for US$550 per month, all 100 units that had been manufactured were rented out almost immediately. Watson Sr saw the writing on the wall and turned over the computer operations to his son.

In 1953, three years before his death, Watson Sr announced the company's first commercially available computer, the IBM 701 (also known as the Defense Calculator). It had all the elements of a real binary computer, including an internal, electric read-write memory. It was 25 times faster than the SSEC but just one-quarter the size. For the first time, IBM was in the computer business.

Meanwhile, the rest of the world wasn't standing still. From Manchester to Tokyo, researchers were developing computer innovations that would make computers powerful enough and user-friendly enough to become irresistible to businesses. Computers were about to blanket the business world.

Before Silicon Valley had silicon chips, a couple of Stanford University electrical engineering students,

Dave Hewlett and Bill Packard, founded Hewlett-Packard in Packard's Palo Alto garage in 1939. (If Packard

had won the coin toss, we'd now know the company as Packard-Hewlett.) Their first product was the 200A

audio oscillator, used to test sound equipment. One of the company's first customers was Walt Disney, who

purchased eight oscillators to test the cinema sound systems that would play *Fantasia*. As the company grew,

the founders developed an open corporate culture – such as offices without doors and non-hierarchical

management – that set a precedent for the entire computer industry in

the decades to come.

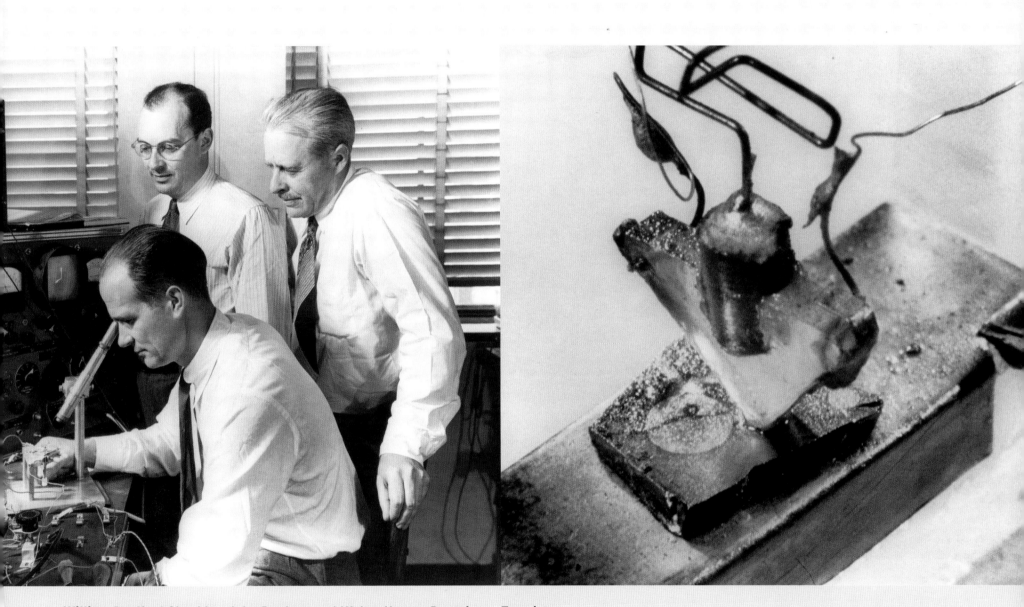

William Bradford Shockley, John Bardeen and Walter Houser Brattain

One of the big problems with computers in the 1940s was that they used vacuum tubes. These were large, expensive, fragile, hot and had a tendency to burn out after a short time. In 1947 three Bell Labs engineers – William Bradford Shockley, John Bardeen and Walter Houser Brattain – invented a device made from germanium, plastic and gold that did everything a vacuum tube could do, only better. In 1949 it got a name: the transfer resistor, or transistor for short. In 1956 the three scientists were awarded the Nobel Prize for their creation. (In later years the lead scientist on the project, Shockley, lost much of his lustre when he tried to promote his theory that black people were intellectually inferior to other races.)

Transistor

You would think that the transistor, a revolutionary amplifier and switch that was superior to the vacuum tube in every way, would have been immediately snapped up by computer makers. But few companies foresaw the potential in those early years. One small Japanese company, Tokyo Telecommunications, scraped together the $25,000 usage fee to incorporate transistors into its products. The investment paid off: in 1956 the company changed its name to Sony.

Core memory

One of the defining aspects of a true computer is its ability to store programmes in memory. In the 1940s vacuum tubes were used as storage, but because they often cost up to US$1,000 each and burned out frequently, they were impractical. In 1949 the physicist in charge of MIT's Whirlwind project, Jay Forrester, started experimenting with a magnetic material called Deltamax and used it to make rings that could switch magnetic polarity when an electrical current was passed through them. The system, called core memory, was an inexpensive and excellent memory storage system and until the 1970s – when semiconductor-based memory chips arrived on the scene – they were the first choice for random access memory.

7320

Drum memory

Before hard disk drives, there were drums. Coated with magnetic material, a drum spun on a motor while a column of magnetic heads read and wrote binary information on the drum. Popular in the 1950s and 1960s, drum memory was replaced by hard disk memory, which was faster and denser. The magnetic drum shown here would have had a storage capacity of about one megabyte. A typical personal computer today has a hard disk drive with a storage capacity of 40,000 megabytes.

IBM's Seletctive Sequence Electronic Calculator (SSEC)

Shortly before the IBM Selective Sequence Electronic Calculator (SSEC) was to be unveiled in a grand ceremony, IBM chairman Thomas Watson Sr toured the room in which it was being housed. "There is just one thing," he said. "The sweep of this room is hindered by those large black columns down the centre. Have them removed before the ceremony." Unfortunately, the columns could not be removed without the building collapsing. IBM's photographs of the room were doctored to remove the columns.

Small-Scale Experimental Machine

Built in 1948 at the University of Manchester, the Small-Scale Experimental Machine (SSEM, affectionately called the "Baby") was the first computer to contain all the components considered to be part of a modern computer. Built by scientists F C Williams and Tom Kilburn, its most notable feature was the ability to store both data and programmes in its electronic memory, called a Williams Tube, which made it much faster than other computers of the same period. It also used drum memory for long-term storage.

Williams Tube

F C Williams and Tom Kilburn devised a way
to store thousands of bits of memory on a
single cathode ray tube, a component that was
being used in radar detection and television at
that time. A Williams Tube was used in the
first electronically stored programme (a 17-
line routine to find the highest factor of a
given number). The Williams Tube was prone
to dropping bits of memory, so it was
eventually replaced with more reliable forms of
volatile memory.

Richard Hamming

To err is human, but when a computer makes a mistake, all hell breaks loose. At the conclusion of the Manhattan Project in 1946, Richard Hamming (1915–1998, above right, with the Rand Corporation's Fred Gruenberger) followed in the footsteps of many other atom bomb scientists: to Bell Labs. There, while writing programmes and using punch cards to load them, he became frustrated by the fact that the computer would frequently make an error when reading a card – it meant he had to resubmit all the cards and cross his fingers that the computer wouldn't misread them again. To save time, he developed an error-detecting and error-correcting code that would self-correct a misread string of binary data. His invention became known as Hamming Code and it is still used in some systems today. With a practical, let's-get-things-done attitude, Hamming was once quoted as saying: "Mathematics is an interesting intellectual sport but it should not be allowed to stand in the way of obtaining sensible information about physical processes."

←| Maurice Wilkes

Already well known for his radio physics work, Maurice Wilkes (b 1913) became the director of the Cambridge Computer Laboratory in 1945. That year he read a pre-publication copy of John von Neumann's proposal for the EDVAC computer (which he had to read overnight, because he had to return it and photocopying machines were almost non-existent) and he decided to model Cambridge's EDSAC (Electronic Delay Storage Automatic Computer) on the same architecture. The computer became a workhorse for the university, and Wilkes became the man in charge of making sure it did what it was supposed to do. He was one of the first to experience the frustration of programmers, as well. He recalls: "As soon as we started programming, we found to our surprise that it wasn't as easy to get programmes right as we had thought. Debugging had to be discovered. I can remember the exact instant when I realized that a large part of my life from then on was going to be spent in finding mistakes in my own programmes."

↑ EDSAC

Unlike other stored programme computers of the era, the EDSAC (Electronic Delay Storage Automatic Computer) was a practical, useful machine. As soon as it was completed in June 1949, it was put to work solving research problems for Cambridge scientists. Similar in both name and operation to John von Neumann's EDVAC, the EDSAC used reliable mercury delay line switches (as opposed to the much faster but dodgy Williams Tube memories), which had been invented by William Bradford Shockley and J Presper Eckert for use in radar systems. Despite a clock speed of just 500 kHz (most personal computers today have clock speeds of a billion Hertz or more) the EDSAC was in constant use and gave rise to the idea of software as being something other than the physical guts, or hardware, of the computer itself.

Whirlwind

Computers in the 1940s were batch-processed machines. That means a programmer would enter the programme, along with the data to be processed, in a stack of cards and load them into a card reader. The card reader would convert the information on the cards into electrical signals, which the computer would process, spitting out the final answer. In other words, there was no interactivity between the user and the computer. But in the Second World War, the US Navy asked MIT to develop a sophisticated flight simulator for bomber crews, and the idea for a real-time, interactive computer was born. Called Whirlwind, it was completed in 1951 and was the first computer with a video display that showed real-time text and graphics. Using Forrester's core memory, Whirlwind was much faster than other computers of the time. The basic architecture of Whirlwind was incorporated into the US Air Force's air defence system, known as SAGE, and the Whirlwind-style computers continued to operate until 1983.

Electronic Control Company

J Presper Eckert and John Mauchly, inventors of the ENIAC, were convinced that computers would become an essential part of business and commerce, so in 1946 they started the Electronic Control Company. After a troublesome start developing a system for the US Census Bureau, they landed a contract with the Northrop Aircraft Company to make a computer to test out ideas about computer-controlled navigation. After that, work started picking up, and in March 1951 Eckert and Mauchly (now working for Remington Rand, which had purchased the Electronic Control Company) unveiled the UNIVAC I (UNIVersal Automatic Computer I), a 13-ton giant that gulped 125 kilowatts of power. In 1952 a UNIVAC, using a sample of 7 per cent of voters, surprisingly (but correctly) picked Eisenhower as the next President of the USA. It launched the machine to instant celebrity status. With a price of about US$1.5 million each, 46 UNIVAC I systems were sold until it was discontinued in 1957.

"Can man build a superman?"

That was the question posed by *Time* on the cover of the 23 January 1950 edition, which featured an anthropomorphic illustration by Boris Artzybasheff of the US Navy's Mark III computer. This was an era in which the media commonly referred to computers as "electric brains" and pondered whether or not computers would replace people as decision makers. In truth, scientists knew that computers were tools – nothing more – which performed the mind-numbing work of crunching numbers, thereby giving humans more time to do real thinking.

ZUSE Z5

Six times faster than the Z4 general purpose computer, which was built in 1944, the Zuse Z5 used telephone relays instead of tubes, which Konrad Zuse considered to be unreliable. The electromechanical Z5 went on sale in 1951, and was quite successful. Some argue that it was the first commercial computer (others say that the Ferranti Mark I holds that honour). Zuse went on to make a number of other noteworthy computers, but by 1964 he had lost ownership and control of his company, and he spent the rest of his life painting.

Ferranti Mark 1

Basically a supercharged Manchester Baby, the Ferranti Mark 1, built in 1951, was the first commercially available general purpose computer. Developed at Manchester University, the Mark 1 also holds the honour of being the first general purpose computer to play chess. The software was written by Dr Dietrich Prinz. Because of the memory and speed limitations, the programme could only play mate-in-two problems and took 15 minutes to make its move. This was an impressive feat, though, considering that the Mark 1 had just 0.0012 megabytes of random-access memory, compared to the 512 megabytes found in today's low-end PCs. Ferranti sold a total of eight Marks. Its first customer was the University of Toronto, which bought one to help engineers design the St Lawrence Seaway.

JOHNNIAC

There seemed to be an unwritten rule that computers made in the 1940s and 1950s had to have names ending in "AC". Witness ENIAC, UNIVAC, SILLIAC, WEIZAC, MANIAC and, in 1953, JOHNNIAC. This computer, built at the Institute for Advanced Study in Princeton, New Jersey, used selectron tubes for storage. (By 1955 the tubes were replaced with core memory, which had become commercially affordable because of cheap Asian labour.) JOHNNIAC's design was informed by the work of John von Neumann, though he disapproved of the name of the computer. Designed for the RAND Institute to help it with analytic studies, JOHNNIAC had a high-speed printer and a "Tablet" – a digitizing surface that could convert a user's pen strokes into binary data. JOHNNIAC ran until 1966.

International Business Machines (IBM)

When the Korean War started in 1950, the US government asked IBM to build a computer to help it design aircraft and nuclear weapons. IBM complied by making

the IBM 701 – "the machine that carried us into the electronics business," said Thomas J Watson, IBM's chairman. Twenty-five times faster than IBM's Selective Sequence Electronic Calculator (SSEC), which was built from 1948, the 701 represented IBM's serious commitment to commercial computers. Four years later, IBM introduced the 704 as an upgrade to the groundbreaking 701. The first mass-produced mainframe computer, it featured floating-point arithmetic, which greatly reduces rounding errors that can accrue when performing arithmetic. From this point onwards, IBM would no longer be considered just a punch-card machine maker, but a

serious contender in the emerging commercial computer industry. Within a few years, it would overtake all its competitors.

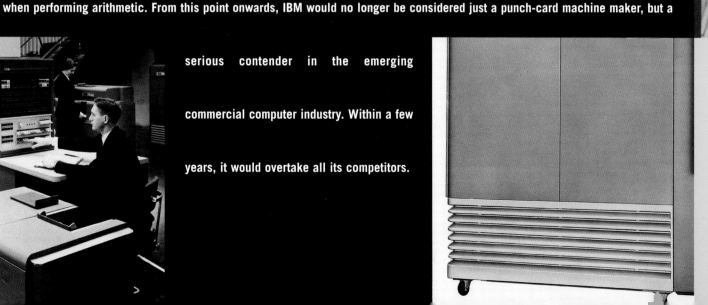

←| ←| IBM 650 Magnetic Drum Calculators

Almost 2,000 IBM 650 Magnetic Drum Calculators were sold between 1953 and 1962, making it the best-selling computer of the 1950s. IBM described it as a "workhorse of modern industry" and a basic system could be rented in 1956 for US$3,750 per month (the price of a luxury automobile at the time), not including the card-punch/card-reader unit, which cost an additional US$550 per month. The 650 also sported an abundance of blinking lights and some historians believe that this was a clever marketing ploy by IBM to show how powerful the machine was.

←| FORTRAN programming language and punch cards

One of the designers of the IBM 701 was John Backus (b 1924), a former researcher at the IBM Watson Laboratory at Columbia University. Backus also oversaw the development of the FORTRAN programming language (official name: IBM Mathematical FORmula TRANslating System), which consumed millions of punch cards during its heyday. Every IBM 701 came with a copy of the FORTRAN compiler and a 51-page programmer's manual. FORTRAN language is still in wide use, because it allows people who know nothing of the inner workings of a computer to get useful work out of it.

IBM 305 RAMAC

In September 1956 IBM introduced the 305 RAMAC (Random Access Method of

Accounting and Control), the first computer to come with a disk drive. Prior to this,

most computers used drums for long-term storage, but drums held just a few kilobytes.

At the request of the US Air Force, which wanted quick access to inventory records at

its Ohio supply depot, IBM designed a disk drive. On 10 February 1954 the first disk

drive in history recorded the sentence: "This has been a day of solid achievement."

Today's laptops have disk drives that measure just over 6 cm (2 ½ in) in diameter and

hold 40,000 megabytes. The RAMAC's drive platters measured 61 cm (24 in) in

diameter and its stack of 50 disks had a capacity of less than 5 megabytes. IBM rented

out the disk drive unit for $35,000 a year.

THE HUMAN BRAIN:

Is science making it obsolete?

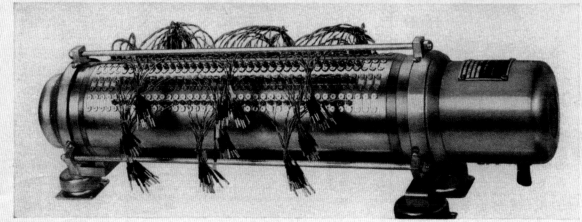

Aɴ intriguing question, particularly so with the development of *electronic* brains — such as the Remington Rand UNIVAC® "memory" drum shown above. The best answer to this question comes from the scientists themselves. It is an unequivocal "no".

Although electronic brains perform many of the routine problem-solving functions of the human brain — and do so with unfailing accuracy, at speeds that are literally inconceivable — electronic brains can never duplicate the higher creative functions of which the mind is capable. On the contrary, by relieving the mind of tedious, time-consuming chores — and supplying it with up-to-the-second information never before obtainable — electronic brains are significantly raising the level of human thinking power.

Aided by Remington Rand UNIVAC, scientists have tracked down the "lost" eighth moon of Jupiter . . . have completed, in a single day, aircraft design research which previously would have taken many years. Government administrators have erased long-standing clerical backlogs *overnight* . . . have reduced census tabulating to a quick, simple, automatic operation.

It is in the world of business, however, that UNIVAC'S real value lies — particularly with the development of the new UNIVAC 60/120 series. This flexible family of computers enables every type of business organization — from the smallest to the very largest — to benefit by the **economy through efficiency** afforded by UNIVAC electronic data-processing.

In modernizing today's office — in helping management to keep costs down—Remington Rand UNIVAC is making an important contribution to business . . . to the economy . . . to our way of life.

Remington Rand UNIVAC, most famous of the electronic brains

. . ."designs" a supersonic wind tunnel   . . .gives sales forecasting an important new dimension: *immediacy*   . . .cuts billing time and paperwork in half!

. . . solves any problem that can be reduced to a formula!

Sputnik I

When the Soviet Union caught the world off guard by launching the first artificial satellite, the Sputnik I, into orbit on 4 October 1957, it kicked off the space race and turned up the heat on the Cold War, both of which demanded faster, better computers. On 31 January 1958 the USA returned the volley by launching the Explorer I satellite, developed by Wernher von Braun (1912–1977) and his staff at Army Redstone Arsenal. The great rocket scientist von Braun was not enamoured of computers, though. He once quipped: "Man is the best computer we can put aboard a spacecraft – and the only one that can be mass-produced with unskilled labour."

⟵| ATLAS

In the mid-1950s at the University of Manchester, Tom Kilburn (1921–2001) started experimenting with

transistors as a replacement for vacuum tubes in computers. With the assistance of Ferranti Ltd,.Kilburn

developed the ATLAS computer in 1962. It was the world's most powerful computer, and was the first computer to

feature virtual memory and a true operating system. It remained in operation until March 1973, supporting more

than 2,000 university projects. Although the ATLAS was a much-used university machine, Kilburn said his work on

the Manchester Baby had more of an emotional impact. In 1992 he said: "The most exciting time was June 1948

when the first [Manchester Baby] worked. Without question. Nothing could ever compare with that."

Integrated circuits

Transistors made vacuum tubes obsolete, and integrated circuits made transistors obsolete. Or more accurately,

integrated circuits shrank transistors and other electronic components down to such a small size that they couldn't be

seen with the human eye. The integrated circuit was invented in 1958 by a Texas Instruments engineer named Jack St

Clair Kilby (b 1923). Using borrowed equipment, Kilby built the first integrated circuit while most of the other employees

at Texas Instruments were taking their two-week vacation. (Kilby had just started working at TI and he wanted to make

a good impression with the boss by working through the holidays.) His invention meant the end of laboriously

hand-soldering components together – and it led to the personal computer revolution. Kilby was also the co-inventor

of the electronic handheld calculator in 1967. Pascal and Leibniz would have been proud.

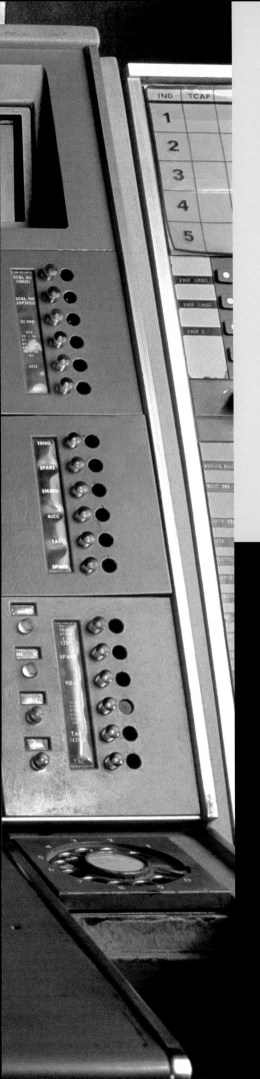

⟵ SAGE system

In the early 1960s 22 SAGE (Semi-Automatic Ground Environment) command centres had been set up by the USA as a radar tracking system for identifying enemy bombers. Costing US$8 billion at the time, the SAGE system was based on the Whirlwind computer developed at MIT. Each SAGE computer weighed 250 tons, had almost 50,000 vacuum tubes and used 3,000 kilowatts of power. Note the built-in ashtray and cigarette lighter. One of the more interesting components was the "light-gun", which looked like a pistol and served the same purpose as a computer mouse (which had yet to be invented). It also had many innovative features that wouldn't be found in other computers for years, such as modem communications and interactivity. Unfortunately, by the time the SAGE system was up and running, the Russians had replaced their bombers with missiles, and SAGE was useless against them. Most of the system was shut down in 1979. One computer, the North Bay system, ran until 1983, and when it was shut down, it was immediately sent to the Computer Museum in Boston and put on display as a Cold War relic.

↓ IBM System/360

Introduced in April 1964, IBM's System/360 computer was decreed by *Fortune* magazine to be IBM's "$5 billion gamble". It was one that paid off for the company and revolutionized the computer industry. Unlike other computers, the System/360 computers were interchangeable with other members of the 360 "family". Any programme that worked on one 360 computer could run on any other model in the 360 line, no matter how large or small. This made it easy for an enterprise to expand its 360 system. The computers also used "solid logic" ceramic modules, which were smaller, faster and more robust than standard transistors. With the introduction of System/360, which was immensely popular within science, government and industry, IBM had won the mainframe wars.

IBM SYSTEM/360

Now one new computer fills all your data processing needs

You can easily increase the size of SYSTEM/360 when your business grows or you want to add new applications.

You don't have to revise most of your programs. You don't have to switch to new input and output devices.

Any program that works on the smallest configuration can work on the largest.

Same goes for the programming systems. The simplest operating system, the simplest language translator or object program can work on any SYSTEM/360.

Same goes for input and output devices. Any printer, tape, storage unit, reader or terminal that works in a small configuration works in a larger one. You choose what you need now. You add new components when you need them.

This is true from the smallest configuration to the largest configuration.

SYSTEM/360 solves today's problems. And it expands to solve tomorrow's problems, too.

It cuts today's costs....and it will also cut tomorrow's. There's never been a system quite like it. IBM DATA PROCESSING

GETTING PERSONAL
GETTING PERSONAL
GETTING PERSONAL
GETTING PERSONAL
GETTING PERSONAL
GETTING PERSONAL
GETTING PERSONAL
GETTING PERSONAL
GETTING PERSONAL
GETTING PERSONAL
GETTING PERSONAL
GETTING PERSONAL
GETTING PERSONAL
GETTING PERSONAL
GETTING PERSONAL
GETTING PERSONAL
GETTING PERSONAL
GETTING PERSONAL
GETTING PERSONAL
GETTING PERSONAL
GETTING PERSONAL
GETTING PERSONAL
GETTING PERSONAL
GETTING PERSONAL
GETTING PERSONAL
GETTING PERSONAL
GETTING PERSONAL
GETTING PERSONAL
GETTING PERSONAL

IBM

In the early 1970s computers were fantastically expensive devices. They were huge, finicky and generated so much heat that they had to be kept in refrigerated rooms. Companies that could afford computers kept them locked away from the employees, who could only peer through plate glass into the computer rooms, filled with whirring tape drives and panels of blinking lights that were comprehensible only to the white-coated experts who maintained the systems. Even the people who used computers to solve problems weren't allowed to touch them. Instead, they handed a stack of punched cards to one of the technicians, whose job it was to serve as an interface between man and machine.

A small, but growing, group of people were unhappy with the way things were. They were typically young engineers who had grown up in a culture that marvelled at the power of computers to do everything from predicting the weather to helping men walk on the moon. While most people would no more think of having a computer in their home than they would a nuclear reactor, this vocal subset – let's call them nerds – desperately wanted computers that they could call their own. They wanted a machine that they could touch, programme and modify. They read magazines like *Popular Electronics* and *Radio Electronics*, which ran articles speculating on the future of home computers. The editor of *Popular Electronics*, Les Solomon, realized that the magazine's readers were desperate for a high-quality home computer. He began searching for someone to design one so he could publish articles about it.

Micro Instrumentation and Telemetry Systems (MITS) was a tiny company located in a shopping precinct in Albuquerque, New Mexico, that had started out in 1968 manufacturing electronic kits for model rocket enthusiasts. In the early 1970s the company's president, Ed Roberts, began selling kits for programmable calculators. But when the calculator market tanked in 1974, Roberts had to come up with an idea to save his company. Luckily, in April of that year Intel announced that it had invented a new microprocessor, called the 8080. After some investigation into the chip's capabilities, Roberts decided that the 8080 would be an excellent core component of a home computer kit. He called Intel and was able to haggle the price of the chip down from US$360 to US$75.

In July Roberts and Solomon met to discuss making the computer kit to sell in *Popular Electronics*. Solomon said that if Roberts was able to make a computer kit costing under US$500, he would guarantee Roberts a cover story and several features in the magazine. For Roberts, this project was his last chance to save MITS, which was US$300,000 in the red. He hoped to sell 200 computer kits, at US$397 each, to make enough money to service his debt until something else came up.

With creditors breathing down his neck, Roberts hastily drew up a basic plan for a microcomputer and handed it over to his two-man engineering department. The plans called for a computer that had room for extra memory, and peripherals such as a Teletype machine.

As the computer was being designed, Roberts asked his employees to suggest names. The best of the bunch was "Little Brother" but Roberts wasn't pleased with it. He contemplated calling it the PE-8 (a short form of Popular Electronics 8080) but that didn't sound right to him, either. A few days before his article deadline, Roberts asked his 12-year-old daughter Lauren if she had any ideas. She told him that the USS *Enterprise* was going to visit a planet called Altair in that evening's episode of *Star Trek*. "Why don't you call it that?" she asked. That's the name Roberts went with.

With the deadline looming, Roberts shipped the one and only Altair computer to the offices of *Popular Electronics* in New York. A couple of days later, he flew out to meet the editors, hoping to show them how the computer worked. But when he arrived, the computer wasn't there. It had been lost during transit because employees of the shipping company were on strike. In a mad scramble, an engineer at MITS put some blinking lights on an empty case and sent it to the magazine. When readers picked up the January 1975 issue of *Popular Electronics*, they had no idea that the computer featured on the cover was an empty box.

The issue heralded a new age for computers, and readers were ecstatic. They were also eager to buy Altair. In the days following the release of the magazine, thousands of orders poured into MITS offices. In less than a month, the company was able to wipe out its US$300,000 debt and take an additional US$250,000 on top of that.

Even though the computer could do little on its own, besides blink its little LEDs, hobbyists loved the Altair and began writing programmes for it. In 1975 two young programmers from Boston telephoned Roberts and asked if he'd be interested in buying a version of the BASIC programming language they wanted to write for the Altair. Roberts was interested, but sceptical. Six months later, the programmers, Bill Gates (aged 19) and Paul Allen (aged 22), flew from Boston to Albuquerque to deliver the software. Soon afterwards, Roberts hired Paul Allen to run MITS's software division, and it wasn't long before Bill Gates joined him.

Unfortunately, success came too soon for the MITS Altair. Orders couldn't be filled fast enough and the promised peripherals, such as keyboard interfaces and tape-drive memory systems that would make the Altair actually useful were put on the back burner. Additional trouble arrived in the form of competition. In 1976 a company called IMS Associates Inc. introduced a computer similar to the Altair, but it came with a monitor, keyboard and floppy disk. In the following months many other competitors introduced computers of their own. Hobbyists had their choice of computer – and they consistently chose one that could do more than make its lights blink. By 1977 MITS was no more. But it will always be remembered as the company that launched the personal computer revolution.

K

RADIO — ELECTRONICS

LATEST IN TELEVISION SERVICING AUDIO

HUGO GERNSBACK, *Editor*

OC 19. 30 U.S. CAN

WORLD'S SMALLEST ELECTRIC BRAIN — SEE ELECTRONICS SECTION

Simon, the first personal computer

Many people think that the first personal computer was created in Silicon Valley in the 1970s, but in fact the credit goes to a company

in Massachusetts called Berkeley Associates, which marketed a home computer model called Simon in 1950. The company's founder, an

insurance analyst named Edmund C Berkeley, had described Simon a year earlier in his book *Giant Brains, or Machines That Think*. With

129 electromechanical relays, Simon could perform simple maths and gave its answers on a row of blinking lights mounted on its casing.

Berkeley sold plans for Simon (the company didn't actually make the computers) and the parts cost around US$500 (about US$3,000 in

today's money). Many personal computer pioneers cut their teeth on Simon. Berkeley also published the first computer magazine, called

Computers and Automation.

BEGINNER'S MANUAL

Experiment # 1.

Simple Circuits.

1) The simplest electric setup you can make is called a circuit which means it forms a circle with electricity moving from where it is to where it isnt.

Here is what a circuit has in it:
A battery which holds electricity.
A switch which turns the electricity on and off.
A bulb that lights when the switch is turned on.

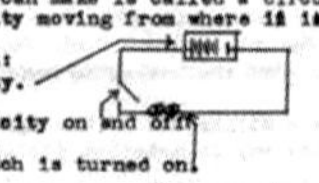

2) Turn to page 60 of your GENIAC MANUAL. Here is a circuit just like the one above but it shows how the special switches work.
The black dots are bolt heads sticking through the panel.
The circles are the rings of little holes.
The little box is a brass jumper on the disc(pp 54-55 MANUAL).
This swings around and lets the electricity move between a bolt in one circle and a bolt in another.
Why do we need these discs? Why not just use knife-blade switches?
First, we need many switches for some experiments and to use the big switches would be very difficult and very expensive. Secondly, we sometimes have to turn on and off several circuits at once. This is done very easily with our discs. In fact that is why they were designed.
Some questions to think about:
How many bulbs can one battery light?
What other things can you put in the circuits in place of bulbs?
What makes a battery work? When yours is worn out, take it apart.
Why does the bulb light when the current flows through it?
Take one apart, but be careful not to cut yourself on the glass.
Draw a picture of what you see. How does the electricity move through the bulb?
You will find the answers to these questions in later experiments.

Experiment # 2.

Series Circuits.

You remember in experiment # 1 we made a simple circuit so that wherever we closed the switch, electricity went from the battery through the bulb and then back again to the battery.
In this experiment we put different things in the circuit to see how much we can make one battery do.

1) Wire up the circuit with two bulbs.
This is the wiring diagram. Of course each bulb must be in a socket.

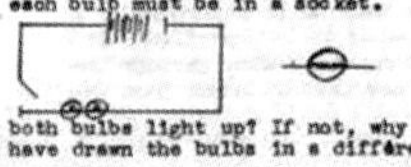

Symbols:
+ Where the electricity is
— Where the electricity isn't
Small coil of wire
→ Direction electricity moves in
Bulb
Battery
Switch

Do both bulbs light up? If not, why not?
We have drawn the bulbs in a different way. Why?

2) Wire up the circuit with three bulbs in series.
Does it still work? If not, why not?

3) Now put two batteries in series so that they are cap to bottom. This puts the + of one next to the — part of another.
Then do experiments # 2 and # 3 again.

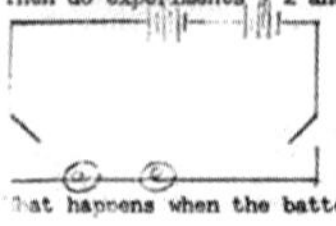

What happens when the batteries have the two + poles facing each other?

4) Does it make a difference if the circuit is wired this way instead of the way in question # 3? If it does, why?

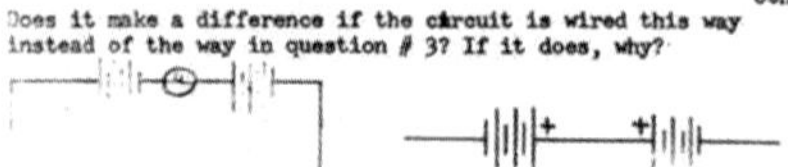

You can now answer some of the questions in experiment # 2. Were you right?

Why are these circuits called series circuits?
Do all bulbs light up equally well?
What makes one bulb shine more brightly than another?
Is it because of the bulb? the place of the bulb in the circuit? or the battery?
Can you make an experiment to answer these questions?
Could you use this circuit to signal over great distances?
What changes would you have to make?

Experiment # 3 — Parallel Circuits.

1) In the diagram below show which way the current flows from the battery and how it comes back again.
Remember current flows from + to —.

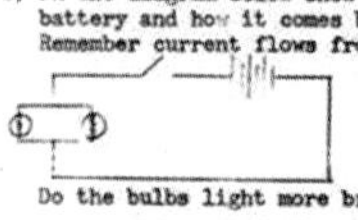

Symbols:
|| Parallel
R Resistance
I Current is amount of elect.

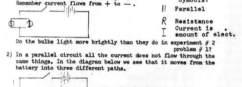

Do the bulbs light more brightly than they do in experiment # 2 problem # 1?

2) In a parallel circuit all the current does not flow through the same things. In the diagram below we see that it moves from the battery into three different paths.

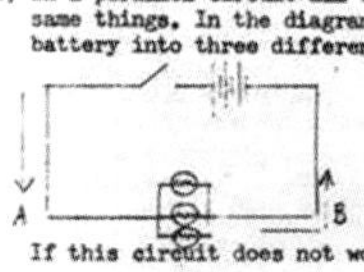

If this circuit does not work, try it with an extra battery.

3) Is there the same amount of current at A and B? At A and C? At A and D? At A and E?
With parallel and series circuits you can design all the circuits used in GENIAC. In fact no more is needed for much more advanced computers.
In subsequent sections of this Beginner's Manual we show you how to use special symbols to describe the circuits and a special algebra to help simplify your first diagrams.

4) Make up your own series parallel circuits with both series and parallel elements in the same circuit. Examine some of the circuits in your GENIAC MANUAL to see what elements they use and how the parallel circuits in particular are used to hold information.

Experiment # 4 — Signalling Circuits.

Signalling Circuit:

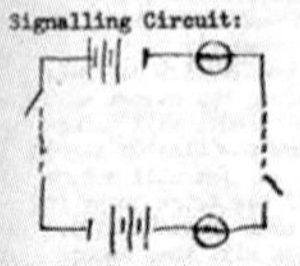

Symbols:
Dot, a quick flash or sound made by closing S.C. and quickly opening it.
Dash, made by holding down the switch longer, then pulling it up.

The little dashes --- mean that you can make the wire as long as you like.
Will the circuit light the bulbs if both switches are open at any one time?
The code most frequently used for signalling in the United States is the MORSE CODE which has a different collection of dots and dashes for each letter. A signal is made either with flash-lights or by having a buzzer sound when you make the current flow.
Remember to keep the batteries + to —.
How long can the wires be with only two batteries?
If you have an Encyclopaedia, look up the MORSE CODE or SAMUEL MORSE, the inventor. How did people send messages over great distances before they had electricity?
Make up your own secret codes to use with friends in GENIAC MANUAL Experiments # 24 and # 25.

Experiment # 5 — Household Wiring.

In your model of a wired up household you will use $1\frac{1}{2}$ volt batteries but your home uses much higher voltages and a different kind of current-alternating current which goes on and off 60 times (cycles) per second. You can see a light flicker as the current rises and falls.
Scale Models of your home lights can be made with the bulbs, sockets and switches in your kit. Up to 10 can be lighted if the circuits are in.
Here is one circuit that was built to light a scale model log cabin.

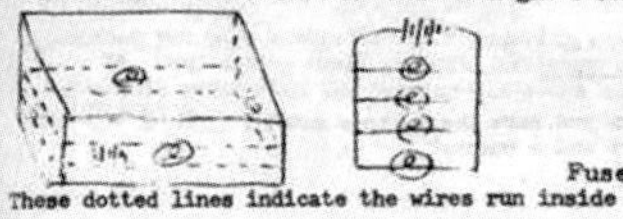

~ Alternating current
Motor
Heater
V=E Volts Electromotive Force
Fuse

These dotted lines indicate the wires run inside the house.

One switch is used. If you want to turn off the lights one by one, loosen them in their sockets. The voltage or maximum push is the sa[me] for each bulb. If each bulb has the same current flowing through it what fraction of the total current flows through each bulb?
Design a circuit that duplicates the wiring in your house.
What is a fuse used for? Go back and take a look at the fuse-box in your house. Before you touch it, make sure your mother or father sh[ows] you how. You can be hurt badly by handling fuses incorrectly. Take [a] look at a spare fuse and describe it. Compare it with a burnt-out f[use].

Experiment # 6 -- Magnetic Fields and Compasses: Electromagnets.

One surprising effect of an electric current is that wherever it mo[ves] it can be detected at a distance. Sometimes this distance is short- as when we tap a telephone, but sometimes we can detect currents al[l the] way around the world, if they have been broadcast properly.
For this experiment you will need a small compass needle. You can m[ake] a compass from a bar magnet. Just rub the needle along the magnet a[nd] place it in a cork floating in a dish of water. The needle will swi[ng] around and fix itself in one direction no matter how the dish is tu[rned].
Now make a small coil of wire and turn the current on. You will not[ice] that the compass needle moves slightly. If the coil has extra loops [it] will affect the compass needle more. Make a tight coil around a nai[l].
This will create a stronger magnetic field. The nail will then beco[me] a magnet test.
How powerful can you make the magnet?
How far away can you detect the electric current flowing?
Can you detect a current flowing in your telephone-line cord?
A loop wrapped around the cord will increase the strength of the si[gnal] amplifying it.

Experiment # 7 -- Bell and Buzzer.

Before we saw how a wire coiled about a piece of iron was made into [a] magnet when the current was turned on. To make a bell or buzzer whi[ch] moves back and forth many times a minute, we fix up the electromagn[et] so that it goes off as soon as it goes on.
Can you do this?
Try to work the diagram out here.
Then make a model of this to test your design.
For a bell you will need some kind of gong and a heavy clapper, but [for] the buzzer you will want a short light piece of metal that moves quickly back and forth.
Here is a diagram that works:

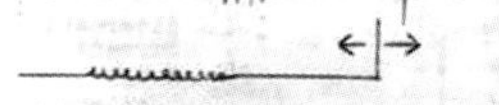

How fast and how often can you make the clapper move?
Can you combine a code key and a buzzer?

Experiment # 8 — Relay Memory.

We now come to a circuit which has a memory!
Stop a minute and think of how your own memory works. Do you remember everything? Or only special things? Do you find that after you have put in extra work remembering something that it stays remembered and is difficult to forget?
Well, this is what a relay does. A relay is just an electromagnet, which is turned on by the current when the current is strong enough. The relay either operates another circuit, or releases when another current flows into the coils on the other side pulling the contact back.
Draw a diagram, then make a relay.
Can you make hook relays in series? in parallels?
How is the remembering in a relay like remembering in the brain?
Which is more certain? Which is more rapid? More complicated?
What other kinds of mechanical memory are there?
What could a human remember that no machine can remember?

Some relay circuits you will find:
Single Pole Single Throw (SPST)
Double Pole Single Throw (DPST)
Single Pole Double Throw (SPDT)
Double Pole Double Throw (DPDT)

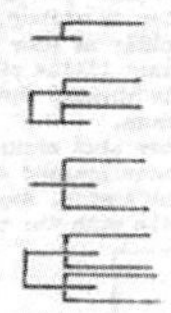

Experiment # 9 — Burglar Alarm.

To design a burglar alarm for your home, decide which windows or doors you expect to be opened. Now rig up a circuit that trips a relay when the window is opened. (See MANUAL EXPERIMENT # 5.)
This means that a little current flows through the magnet of the relay which in turn causes a much larger current to flow. This is an important idea. We are really making the current larger or amplifying it by letting a little current "tickle" a larger current into action. Just in the same way a little bit of dust makes us shake with sneezes.
You should be able to design this circuit yourself:
Step 1: Make up the black boxes that will stand for machines that do certain things.

Burglar Alarm [ ] + Relay [ ] gives → Signal [ ]
Just a circuit that sends a current when the window opens
Can be a bell or buzzer

Whenever you have a circuit you think will work, make a model and test it. Keep trying until you get just what you want.
The actual wiring for the burglar alarm can be seen in MANUAL EXPERIMENT # 5.

Experiment # 10 — Question-answering Game.

The principle of the questionnaire is this:

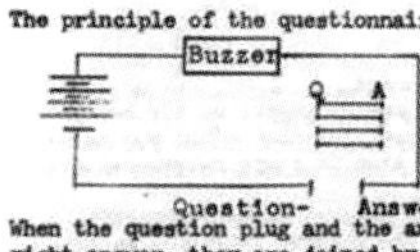

When the question plug and the answer plug are connected to the right answer, they are joined by a length of wire.
This is clue enough. If you are still puzzled, take a look at any Electric Game to see how it works.

Experiment # 11 — Telephone.

The telephone is just a wire carrying a voice. You can make a telephone without electricity, but they carry further with it.
To make an electric telephone you create an electric current that is strong when your voice is strong, weak when your voice is weak, and changes just as rapidly as your speech does.
One way is to talk against little pieces of carbon through which a current is passing. This changes the resistance as your voice hits it— loud voice less resistance.
Try to devise a telephone that works with a different mechanism. Take advantage of what you have learned so far. Examine your own phone. Unscrew the cup and look inside. Replace it and put it back as you found it to avoid trouble with the telephone company.

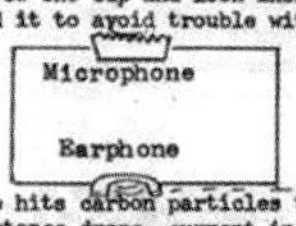

Voice hits carbon particles through which current is passing. Current resistance drops, current increases.
At the other end this increased current causes the plate in the earphone to vibrate more rapidly, reproducing the original sound.

Experiment # 12.

We are now going to use a new method for describing some simple experiments that appear in the GENIAC MANUAL.
This method is called Boolean Algebra and is used by computer engineers to simplify their circuit networks. Boolean Algebra operates like ordinary algebra, but is different from it. Ordinary algebra is concerned with numbers, Boolean Algebra is interested in states or conditions.
For example:
Experiment # 12 (# 1 in your MANUAL).
Problem: Describe in symbols the various states in which a simple on-off switch can exist.
Condition ON, switch is closed, current flowing, Condition O
Condition OFF, switch is open, current not flowing, Condition I
We could call Condition O - a or x or p and
Condition I - a'(for non-a) or x'(for non-x) or p'(for non-p).

In describing states of different combinations of equipment we can use any set of letters or numbers that are useful to us.
Experimental: If a switch closed is O and open is I, describe the switch arrangement symbolically in MANUAL EXPERIMENT # 2.

Experiment # 13.

In experiment # 12 you were asked to describe the MANUAL EXPERIMENT called "Hall Lights" in symbols.
One solution is:
O plus O means both switches are closed.
I plus I means both switches are open.
Plus means they are in series. A dot between two numbers means they happen at once, or are in parallel.
Thus for O · O you read " A closed circuit in parallel with a closed circuit is a closed circuit". ——— O · O = O
Read " An open circuit in series with an open circuit is an open circuit". ——— I · I = I
Write out the meanings of the following equations:
I + O = O + I = I
O · I = I · O = O
O + O = O
I · I = I

Experiment # 14.

Before we go further in the problem of describing more complicated circuits we can see that system of O I for on and off is all that is necessary in building computer circuits to add, subtract, multiply or divide with digital computers. We are primarily interested in whether the circuit is on or off. Much like the game of Twenty Questions Yes or No is sufficient direction when combined in the proper series of questions to allow you to identify any object. If we signify Yes by O and No by I, we can find the answer to a variety of questions. Look for example at experiment # 11 in your MANUAL, the machine for Douglas MacDonald's Will. We can sort out the different cases into recombinations in a variety of Yes-No answers. The machine's wiring diagram (see Wiring Diagram Manual) just carries out the arrangement of the schematic's easily moved parts.
In this experiment you can see without too much difficulty how to set up the wiring directly from the problem at hand.
Experimental: Choose another paragraph with complicated material in it, your own life insurance policy is a good example, and set the contents in a schematic diagram after the paradigm on page 16. Then set up a pattern of switches to handle the information and lights to give you an asnwer. You will have to correlate the wiring in #11 (MANUAL) with the schematic to understand how your own machine should be built up. Once you have sketched out the wiring, you can simplify it.

Experiment # 15.

We can write a set of yes-no answers as follows: (from Experiment # ...
A (shut-open) O I Zero and I correspond to the state of being shut [and] open. No further significance should be attached [to] these numbers.
B (on-off) O I
C (zero-full) O I
Then OOO or O for switch A and zero for switcn B and zero for switch [C] will light bulb 2.
OOI light 1
OIO light 3
OII light 3
IIO,III light 4
IOI,IOO light 3
This becomes a convenient way of summarizing a complicated description. That it also is the binar[y] for certain numbers is only incidentally important
We can describe all the states that exist with only 3 positions and two numbers O and I.
Once your machine is set up you can introduce a variety of other mechanical problems involving three problems by substituting new lab[els] for the old ones. All of these can incorporate three variables in tw[o] positions. Furthermore, you can connect the output of the circuits t[o] do useful work, besides just lighting bulbs, e.g. a rain alarm that [...] when a conducting plastic strip is moistened. A becomes "if you are [in] the house (in-out)" and is connected to the front hall light switch [or] door latch. B dial is window (open-shut), C "plastic trigger" (avail[able] from Science Kits) has extra moisture above dew level on it.

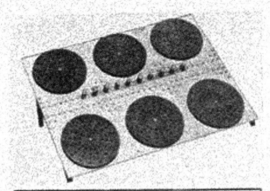
Geniac

In 1955 Berkeley began selling a build-it-yourself computer called the Geniac Electric Brain Construction Kit for US$17.95. With more than 400 components (mainly wires, light bulbs, clips, nuts and bolts) and a 64-page manual, it allowed hobbyists to build "over 30 small electric brain machines that reason arithmetically or logically, play games, including Nim and Tit-Tac-Toe, solve puzzles, etc," according to an advertisement. It was a very popular kit in the 1950s and sold well. In 1958 a book called *The Space Child's Mother Goose* included a poem about the Geniac, describing it as a "Digital miracle, Giving an answer that's Truly empirical".

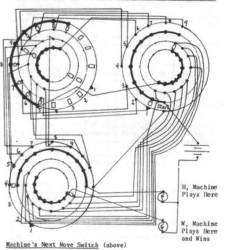

Following is the circuit diagram (in the form of a tem-
plate, showing the rear or wiring side):

Player's Current Move Switch: Machine's Last Move Switch:

H, Machine Plays Here

W, Machine Plays Here and Wins

Machine's Next Move Switch (above)

All wipers are shown with the switch in the No. 1 position. Note the special arrangement of wipers on the Player's
Current Move Switch.

– 38 –

Heathkit EC-1

The Heathkit EC-1 was an analogue computer for educational use. Introduced in 1960 for US$400, the EC-1 used amplifiers to vary output voltage. Heathkit's advertising literature described the computer as an "Excellent teaching aid for a course in computer electronics – Vividly illustrates the electronic analogies to mathematical problems – Handles problems as complex as fluid flow, damped harmonic motion, and flight of a projectile in a viscous medium". By 1965 digital computers had taken over the market and the EC-1 was relegated to the back shelf of computing curiosities.

Minivac 601

Advertised as "the small electronic brother of the huge electronic brains that are the newest tools of science and industry", the Minivac 601 was invented by famed information theorist Claude Shannon and introduced by the Scientific Development Corporation in 1961 for US$85. With six telephone relays, it could be programmed to play tic-tac-toe, among other games, and could generate random numbers.

The first computer mouse

In 1964 Doug Engelbart, a scientist at the Stanford Research Institute (SRI) in Menlo Park, California, was engrossed in a long-term project to "augment human intellect". As part of his research, he wanted to make a hand-operated device to interact with computer displays. At the time, light pens and joysticks were being used, but Englebart felt that these were too cumbersome or didn't offer enough control. He made the first computer mouse out of wood, putting the cord on the front (the next version moved the cord to the back of the mouse). Englebart says SRI patented the mouse, but didn't realize its value. SRI eventually licensed the mouse to Apple for just US$40,000. Today, more than 400 million people use a mouse to control their computers.

Graficon

In the early 1960s Engelbart tested a variety of "pointing" peripherals to work with his graphic user interface designs, including mice, light pens, knee-operated controllers and track balls. Shown here, the Graficon was one of the pointing devices that ended up losing out to the mighty mouse. By 1968 Engelbart and his team of researchers at SRI had invented or integrated many of the revolutionary computer interface elements, such as hypertext and videoconferencing, which would fuel the personal computer revolution.

Digital Equipment Corporation PDP-8

Mainframe computers took a step up by getting smaller, in 1965, with the introduction of the Digital Equipment Corporation (DEC) PDP-8, the first popular minicomputer. The smallest model could fit in the trunk of a car and DEC's salesmen would sometimes deliver them to customers that way. Using transistors and core memory, the US$18,000 PDP-8 was much less powerful than an IBM mainframe, but it was easy to use and it was affordable – companies that couldn't otherwise afford an IBM computer bought a PDP-8. By 1966 DEC had sold 400 PDP-8s, and in the next ten years more than 30,000 systems were sold.

↑ ↦ Honeywell Model 316 Kitchen Computer

The cover of the 1965 Neiman-Marcus catalogue had a picture of a pleased housewife gazing at a bright red piece of furniture that looked like a Saarinen-designed keyboard synthesizer. It was the Honeywell Model 316 Kitchen Computer, a US$10,600 device that did little more than store recipes (it also had a cutting board mounted in the surface). The advertisement stated: "If she can only cook as well as Honeywell can compute." The H316 came with just 4K of memory. Not a single person ordered a Kitchen Computer from Neiman-Marcus, which isn't surprising. After all, who wants a 68 kg (150 lb) monstrosity in the middle of the kitchen, when a stack of recipe cards could do more, take up less space and cost about 25 cents?

⟵ Intel

In 1968 Bob Noyce and Gordon Moore, a couple of engineers at Fairchild Semiconductor, quit their jobs to start a new semiconductor company in Silicon Valley. They approached a San Francisco venture capitalist who, upon reading Noyce's one-page business plan, gave them US$2.5 million to start the Intel Development Corporation. Intel made history when it produced the first single-chip microprocessor, the Intel 4004, in 1971. This integrated circuit contained all the essential components of a computer – the central processing unit, input and output controls, and memory – on a single chip, making the personal computer revolution possible. Today, Intel is the largest manufacturer of microprocessors in the world. Shown here are Gordon Moore (left), CEO of Intel from 1975 to 1987, and Andy Grove (right), CEO from 1987 to 1998, and current chairman.

⟼ Steve Wozniak

Steve Wozniak fits the original definition of a hacker – not someone who breaks into computer systems to wreck them, but a person who pushes technology beyond its limits to come up with something that no one else has thought of. As a child, he built crystal radios and a tic-tac-toe machine. In 1962, when he was 13 years old, he designed a transistor calculator and entered it in a science fair. He won first prize. In 1971 he developed a computer with a friend, Bill Fernandez, and called it the Cream Soda Computer (so named because they drank a lot of the stuff while they were making it). In 1969, Wozniak had met Steve Jobs, five years his junior. Jobs was also an electronics hobbyist and the two hit it off immediately. Soon they were selling "blue boxes" – illegal devices that could be used to make free long-distance calls from payphones. They sold almost 150 blue boxes, at prices ranging from US$40 to US$150 each. Seven years later, on 1 April 1976, the pair of friends founded Apple Computer.

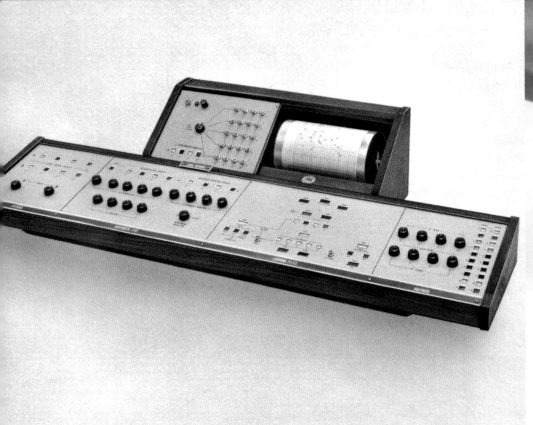

The Arkay CT-650

In 1967 Edward Alcosser, James P. Phillips and Allen M. Wolk wrote a book titled *How to build a Working Digital Computer*. The amazing thing about this visionary book is that diligent readers could build a real working computer — with drum memory — out of household components, such as tin cans and paperclips. No transistors or tubes were required. The computer became known as the "Paperclip Computer". In 1969 the Comspace company developed a computer based on the one described in this book, and called it the Arkay CT-650. It sold for $1,000.

The floppy disk

In the 1960s computers stored data on hard drives (which were very expensive) or reel-to-reel tape (which was less expensive but very slow). But in 1971 IBM introduced the floppy disk, which it called the "memory disk". The 20 cm (8 in) plastic disk was coated with magnetic material, on to which data could be read and written. In 1976 the more familiar 14 cm (5 ¼ in) floppy drive was developed and it quickly became the standard storage method for the first personal computers. In 1981 the 14 cm (5 ¼ in) floppies moved aside for the smaller and more capacious 9 cm (3 ½ in) floppies. Today, most computers don't come with floppy drives, since data can be transferred more easily over a network or burned on to a DVD.

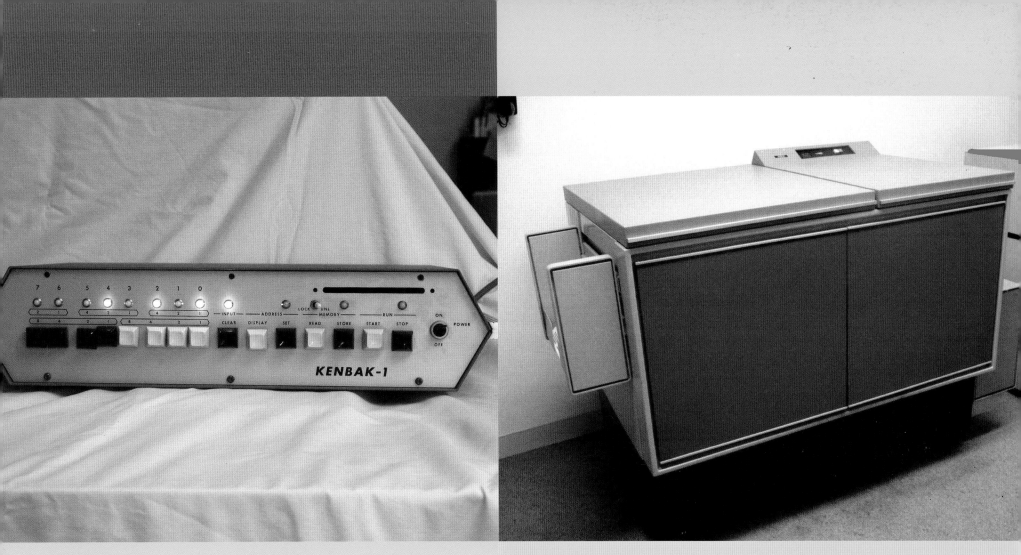

Kenbak-1

With 256 bytes of memory, the Kenbak-1 was introduced to the world by its inventor John Blankenbaker with an advertisement in the September 1971 issue of *Scientific American*, promising that "Very quickly you, or your family or students can write programmes of fun and interest". Although it didn't use a microprocessor, this US$750 kit computer is considered by the Computer History Museum to be the first true personal computer, because it was the first low-cost "von Neumann"-style computer. Blankenbaker sold about 40 Kenbak-1s until he closed the company in 1973.

The laser printer

Xerox tried to stop Gary Starkweather from inventing the laser printer. When he conceived of the idea, in 1967, lasers cost about US$3,000 and that was too much for Xerox. His boss told him to stop working on the project, but he forged ahead without letting anyone other than his closest confidants know about it. Fortunately, in 1970, when Xerox founded the Palo Alto Research Center, Starkweather came to them with his idea and because they were looking for a high-end printer for their computer project, they gave him the go-ahead. In 1973 Starkweather had a working prototype and in 1977 Xerox introduced the model 9700, the first commercial laser printer. But when Starkweather asked to develop a laser printer for personal computers, he was rebuffed. Meanwhile, Hewlett-Packard picked up the ball and, in 1980, introduced the first personal laser printer. HP has since sold more than 30 million laser printers.

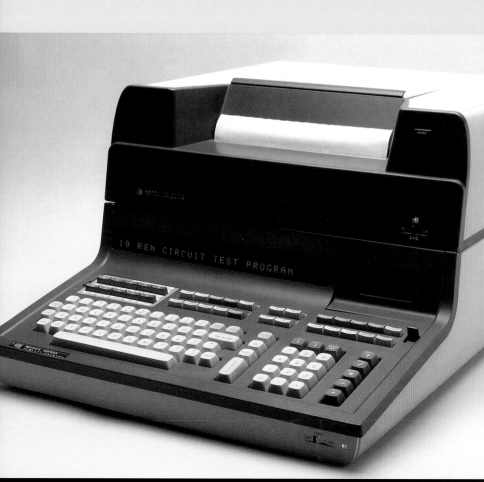

↑ **Hewlett-Packard 9830A**

Introduced in 1972 at a price of US$5,975, the Hewlett-Packard 9830A was like a calculator on steroids. It came with the BASIC programming language and, for an additional US$10,945, you could get a 2.4 megabyte hard disk drive for it. While this was quite expensive, the 9830A was the closest thing to a real personal computer at the time. It could be attached easily to a plotter and it became a favourite device for computer enthusiasts, who would sneak into work at night and at the weekend to programme games and graphics on it.

←| **Traf-O-Data…**

Psst – wanna hot stock tip? Hop in a time machine and invest a couple of thousand in a company called Traf-O-Data, located in a dorm room at Washington State University, circa 1972. It's run by a couple of college students and they've got a killer idea – a device to count holes in paper tape for automobile traffic analysis. Oh wait, scratch that. Traf-O-Data went bust when the State of Washington started offering free tape counting. Instead, wait a year and invest your money in these two kids' other company, a software firm that sells programming languages for hobbyists' personal computers. Remember the name: it's called Microsoft.

Xerox PARC

The title of a book about the history of Xerox's Palo Alto Research Center (PARC) sums it up nicely: *Fumbling the Future: How Xerox Invented, Then Ignored, the First Personal Computer.* Written by Douglas K Smith and Robert C Alexander, and published in 1988, the book details how Xerox, which had made a fortune in the copier machine business, didn't know how to capitalize on its even bigger invention – the personal computer, the graphical user interface and the personal laser printer. Because of poor management decisions at Xerox, the innovations at PARC were adopted by other computer makers (most notably Apple) and Xerox lost out on the fortunes made in the personal computer business.

⟵ Xerox PARC Alto

When Xerox PARC produced its first Alto computer in 1975, it looked like something that might have been dropped by aliens. It had 128KB of memory, a windows-based graphical user interface, proportional font display, a mouse, a laser printer and the ability to network with other computers. It was, in short, almost exactly like the first Macintosh computer, which wouldn't make its debut for another nine years. It's not surprising that the Macintosh resembled the Alto so closely – in 1979 Steve Jobs visited Xerox PARC and was blown away by the system. He eventually hired some PARC engineers to help develop the Lisa and Macintosh computers. In later years, when Apple sued Microsoft for violating the Macintosh operating system's "look and feel", Microsoft's defence amounted to "we both stole it from the Alto".

⟼ Jon Titus's Mark 8

The cover of the July 1974 issue of *Radio-Electronics* had a photograph of the first personal computer kit that used a microprocessor. Inside the magazine, inventor Jon Titus described his Mark 8 computer and offered complete plans (US$5) to build one of your own for about US$350. He would also sell you the printed circuit boards on which you could solder the components. The Mark 8 inspired the formation of many amateur computer building clubs around the USA and Europe. In all, Titus sold about 75,000 sets of plans and 400 board sets.

Creative Computing magazine

Launched in June 1974, *Creative Computing* was the first computer magazine aimed at general readers. During its decade-long run, founder David Ahl (a former employee of the minicomputer maker Digital Equipment Corporation) presented readers with a cornucopia of computer gaming, art and problem solving. Every issue contained complete programmes for games, mazes and other applications written in BASIC, which users could key in by hand. People would spend hours laboriously typing in programmes from the magazine, in order to play simple shoot-'em-ups, or print out Snoopy pictures. Today, copies of the magazine are highly sought after by retrocomputing enthusiasts.

Homebrew Computer Club

On 5 March 1975 the first meeting of the Homebrew Computer Club was called to order in Gordon French's garage in Menlo Park, California. Hobbyists exchanged components, programmes and plans for computers. Word quickly spread about the Homebrew club, and by the third meeting, several hundred people showed up at French's garage. The meetings were moved to a bigger venue. Within a year the club had more than 750 members, including the not-yet-famous Steve Jobs and Steve Wozniak, who showed off a computer they called the Apple I at one of the meetings.

Steve Jobs

Born in 1955, Steve Jobs was adopted and grew up in Silicon Valley. His father was a machinist at Spectra-Physics and he credits his father's work as an inspiration. During the summer of his thirteenth year he worked at Hewlett-Packard, where he met 18-year-old Steve Wozniak. The two became best friends, making and selling "blue boxes" (illegal devices to make free phone calls) together. In 1974 Jobs went to work full-time for Atari as a video game designer, then left for a soul-searching trip to India. When he came back in 1975, he and Wozniak began attending the Homebrew Computer Club meetings together, where they showed off the Apple I, which they'd designed in Jobs's parents' house (shown here) in their spare time.

Altair 8800

When the Altair 8800 was introduced in March 1975, it took the members of the Homebrew Computer Club by storm. It was the computer to have, even though it wasn't much to look at. The base model came with just 256 bytes of random access memory – that's 0.25 kilobytes, barely enough to store the text of this paragraph – and programming it required the user to flip switches on and off. Output was limited to a row of blinking red lights. MITS (the company in Albequerque, New Mexico, that made the Altair) sold it in kit form for US$395, or US$495 ready-assembled. More than 5,000 were sold in the first year. Of course, computer enthusiasts soon figured out how to add a keyboard and monitor to the Altair to make it more useful. Today, an Altair 8800 sells for US$1,200 in collectors' circles.

IBM 5100

In 1975, six years before it introduced the PC, IBM made the 5100 portable computer. With a healthy 16 kilobytes of memory and an integral 12.7 cm (5 in) monitor, keyboard and tape drive, 5100 was a true stand-alone personal computer. However, its base price of US$8,975 make it unaffordable to home users. Also, it weighed 23 kg (50 lb) so the machine was anything but portable – unless you compared it to the great iron beasts that preceded it.

Apple I

When Steve Wozniak designed the Apple I computer in 1976, he had no idea that his little machine would ignite a fire that would soon cover the world. Like the Altair, it had no keyboard or monitor. It didn't even have a power supply – it was a true hobbyists' machine. Apple I had a sales price of US$666.66, and Jobs and Wozniak made 200 units, 100 of which were purchased by a Bay Area computer store called The Byte Shop. In the first ten months, Apple had sold 175 units and users had learned how to add keyboards, monitors, tape drives and printers to the Apple I. They also developed useful programmes for it, such as a payroll application. The Apple I Owners' Club, which formed shortly after the computer was released, is still active.

⟵| Apple II

With the introduction of the Apple II on 5 June 1977, Apple Computer was clearly the company to beat. The Apple II had the ability to hold 64KB of memory, a built-in keyboard, seven slots to accommodate expansion cards and an out-of-the-box ease of use. It soon became the company's flagship product. The Apple II was also able to display colour graphics, an awesome feat at the time. In early 1978 Apple released a floppy disk drive, the Apple Disk II, which was much faster and more convenient than tape recorder data-storage systems. Apple continued to produce Apple II models until 1992. By that time, the Macintosh had won the hearts and minds of most Apple users.

Commodore PET

Commodore was just one of many calculator manufacturers, until it introduced the Commodore PET (Personal Electronic Transactor) in January 1977 at the Consumer Electronics Show in Chicago, Illinois. The PET was an enormously popular personal computer and buyers had to wait months to get one. It came with a keyboard, a 23 cm (9 in) blue-and-white monitor, a power supply and a cassette-tape storage system. With its built-in BASIC programming language interpreter (written by Bill Gates himself) and true graphics capability, users could, and did, programme all manner of applications on their beloved PETs. In the late 1970s PET users could subscribe to a cassette-tape-based "magazine" called *Cursor*. Each issue contained several new game and utility programmes for the PET.

Tandy/Radio Shack TRS-80

Affectionately dubbed the "Trash 80", the Tandy/Radio Shack TRS-80 went on sale in Radio Shack's retail outlets around the USA in 1977 for US$599. The microprocessor and other circuitry were placed under the keyboard and the black-and-white monitor was placed on the desktop behind it. Only 3,000 examples were made in the first production run because the company was afraid that customers might balk at the price. (It was the most expensive product in the store.) However, 10,000 people ordered a TRS-80 Model I within a month, and 55,000 were sold in the first 12 months. Tandy went on to achieve sales of a quarter of a million of the TRS-80 Model I. It was discontinued shortly after Tandy introduced the all-in-one Model III (shown here) in July 1980.

← VisiCalc

The idea of a "killer app" – a computer programme that is so great people will buy a computer just to use it – was born when Dan Bricklin and Bob Frankston created VisiCalc, the first computer spreadsheet, for the Apple II computer in 1979. The programme was nothing short of revolutionary. It made it easy for anyone to create number-intensive analyses that could be automatically updated with the press of a key. VisiCalc's cellular approach to data analysis was original and brilliant – and it proved more than anything that personal computers had a place in homes and small businesses. Shown here is Daniel Fylstra, of VisiCorp, which marketed VisiCalc with an IBM PC XT (left) running VisiON and an Apple II (right) running VisiCalc.

↑ Clive Sinclair

Call him "Mister Miniature". After a stint as an editor for *Practical Wireless*, Clive Sinclair started an electronics company, Sinclair Radionics Ltd, in 1961. In 1966 he introduced a pocket television called the Sinclair Microvision, shown here, and in 1972 he introduced one of the first pocket calculators, the Sinclair Executive, which sold for £69 (US$130). In 1978 Sinclair began selling a computer in kit form called the MK 14 (Microcomputer Kit 14). It sold well, so he made a tiny and inexpensive home computer, called the ZX80, in January 1980. He sold 20,000 and in the next year introduced a more powerful version, the ZX81.

Apple Lisa

Shortly after Steve Jobs had seen a demo of a computer with a graphical user interface (GUI) at Xerox PARC in 1979, he went to work on making one for Apple. He dubbed it the Lisa, which stands for either "Local Integrated Software Architecture" or the name of his daughter, born in 1978. Apple spent US$50 million and four years developing the Lisa, but when it was finally introduced, it flopped. The microprocessor in the US$9,995 Lisa was just not up to the task of handling the intensive number crunching required to support a GUI. Around this time, Jobs was gently pushed away from the Lisa by people who felt that he was too brusque and he became interested in another project at Apple. This project was headed up by Jef Raskin, who wanted to make a low-cost GUI computer, which he'd named after his favourite type of apple, the Macintosh. In short order, Jobs pushed Raskin aside and took over the project.

↑ Sinclair ZX80

When it was brought to market in 1980, the ZX80 computer was the smallest and cheapest home computer in the world. It measured 23 cm by 17.8 cm (9 in by 7 in) and sold for £99.95 (US$190), or £79.95 (US$150) in kit form. To keep the cost down, inventor Clive Sinclair endowed the ZX80 with a novel "membrane"-style keyboard. Despite its diminutiveness, the ZX80 and its descendants were enormously popular in the UK and the USA – Sinclair sold 300,000 ZX81s, and in 1983 he was selling 12,000 ZX Spectrums per week.

Osborne 1

In 1980 Adam Osborne, a British technology journalist living in the USA, started the Osborne Computer Company. He hired one of the most revered members of the Homebrew Computer Club to design a low-cost portable computer, the Osborne 1. The computer made its debut in April 1981 at the seventh West Coast Computer Faire in San Francisco. When several Apple employees stopped by the Osborne booth, Osborne is said to have remarked: "The Osborne 1 is going to outsell the Apple II by a factor of 10, don't you think so?" before adding: "Go back and tell Steve Jobs that the Osborne 1 is going to outsell the Apple II and the Macintosh combined!". When Jobs heard of Osborne's boasting, he immediately called the Osborne Computer Corporation and asked to speak to Osborne. The secretary told Jobs that Mr Osborne was out for the day, but would he like to leave a message? "Yes", said Jobs. "Here's my message. Tell Adam he's an arsehole."

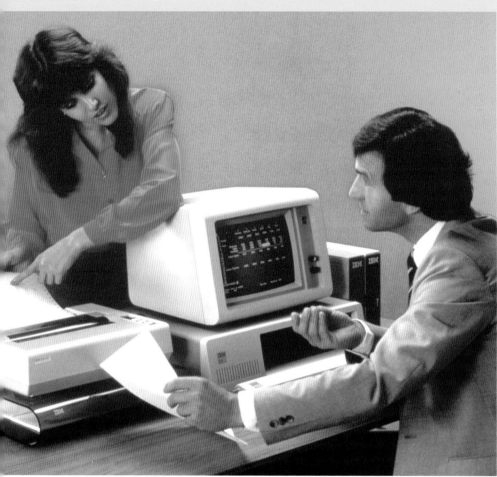

↑ IBM PC

Perhaps the most well-known personal computer of all, the IBM PC was introduced on 12 August 1981. Expandable to 256KB of memory and with a 160KB floppy disk drive, the US$1,565 PC was based in part on the much more expensive IBM 5150. It represented a somewhat desperate move by IBM to gain some of the market share that Apple had taken with its Apple II. A group of 12 people at IBM worked for a year to rush the PC to market, using off-the-shelf components to avoid the long lead times inherent in the development of original parts. IBM also allowed other companies to produce "clone" computers that would run the same software. IBM would receive a royalty on each clone sold. The trouble was that competitors learned how IBM's PC worked and developed IBM-compatible machines that were exempt from royalties. Nevertheless, the PC was a success, because, as the saying goes: "No one ever got fired for buying IBM".

↦ Osborne 1

The first truly portable computer was the Osborne 1, a "transportable" computer,

introduced in April 1981. It had 64KB of memory, built-in floppy drives, a tiny

11.5 cm (4 ½ in) monitor and a built-in word processor, but the US$1,795, 10.4 kg

(23 ½ lb) Osborne was missing one thing everyone wants in a portable computer: a battery.

In order to use the Osborne I, you had to plug it into a wall outlet. Nevertheless, the

Osborne sold well, until company boss Adam Osborne began boasting in 1983 about how

much better the Osborne II was going to be. Would-be customers immediately stopped

buying the Osborne I because they wanted to wait for the Osborne II to come out. The

cashflow interruption sent the company into a tailspin from which it never recovered.

Osborne Computer filed for bankruptcy on 13 September 1983.

← Xerox Star 8010

The Xerox Star 8010, a production version of the Xerox PARC Alto, may have been light years

ahead of other computers when it was introduced on 27 April 1981, but at a price of

US$16,595, hardly anyone could justify the cost – even if it meant being able to boast of owning

the only computer around with a graphical user interface, a mouse, networking and a high-

resolution 43 cm (17 in) monitor. Without a doubt, the Star 8010 was a stunning computer, but it

was simply too far ahead of its time. Apple, with its Macintosh, was right on time in 1984.

(Microsoft, on the other hand, was way behind – its first usable graphical user interface,

Windows 3.0, wasn't released until 1990.)

↦ BBC Micro

After the BBC produced and aired a well-received documentary about the microcomputer revolution ("The Mighty Micro") it decided to capitalize on its success

by developing a personal computer for the education market. The BBC wanted to be able to use the computer in conjunction with its 1981 television series

The Computer Programme. The company first approached Clive Sinclair, but the negotiations ground to a halt after Sinclair was unable to deliver a computer

based on the BBC's needs. The BBC then turned to a small company named Acorn, made up of students from Cambridge University, to develop the computer,

called the BBC Micro. When the computer was released, Acorn and the BBC hoped to sell 12,000 Micros but they actually sold in excess of one million.

Commodore C64

The first Commodore C64 personal computer was introduced in September 1982 for US$595. By the time the last one rolled off the production line, in 1993, some 30 million C64s had been sold. The C64 came with a beefy 64KB of memory, making it an instant favourite with people who wanted to write and play games on it. The C64 also had a synthesizer chip, so it could play sophisticated sounds. In 1984 Commodore made a critical mistake when it released the Commodore Plus/4, which came with a better colour monitor, because it could not run any of the thousands of programmes written for the original C64. Commodore made up for the error by making sure its follow-up models were compatible with programmes from the enormous library of older C64 software titles.

↦ John Sculley

John Sculley will be forever remembered as the man who fired Steve Jobs. In 1983 Sculley was an executive at Pepsi Cola when Jobs asked him to become president. Jobs put it this way: "You can stay and sell sugar water or you can come with me and change the world."

Sculley opted to change the world. But when Jobs's pet project, the Mac, failed to meet sales expectations in 1985 and Apple posted its first-ever quarterly loss, Sculley went to Apple's board. He told them that if they didn't back up his demand to take Jobs off the Macintosh division, he would tender his resignation. The board backed him. In disgust, Jobs quit Apple and sold all his stock. Sculley oversaw the development of the Macintosh II. Sales were phenomenal, and for the next several years, Apple did phenomenally well as a company. Sculley felt vindicated.

"Man of the Year", 1982

In 1982 *Time* magazine broke with tradition by giving the personal computer its "Man of the Year" award. It was the first time an object had been recognized in this way. In an article entitled "The Computer Moves In", *Time* stated: "There are some occasions… when the most significant force in a year's news is not a single individual but a process, and a widespread recognition by a whole society that this process is changing the course of all other processes." According to a survey that *Time* conducted that year, 80 per cent of Americans polled "expect that in the fairly near future, home computers will be as commonplace as television sets or dishwashers".

Apple Macintosh

Even though it represents just one out of every 33 personal computers in homes and businesses, the Macintosh is famous. But when Apple introduced the first Macintosh, in January 1984, it was nearly a flop. Yes, it was the first affordable computer to come with a mouse, a sophisticated graphical user interface and a 32-bit microprocessor (most personal computers of the day were limping by on just eight bits), but it was also deeply flawed. For one thing, the operating system consumed so much of its 128KB memory that there was little room left over for running other applications. Its lack of a hard drive was exacerbated by the fact that it had only one floppy drive, so copying a disk was tedious. In truth, the first Macintosh almost killed the company. But subsequent models were much better and the Mac of today is an exemplar of computing sophistication and elegance.

Andy Hertzfeld and Bill Atkinson

A great deal of the Macintosh's design and interface were the product of two men, Bill Atkinson (right) and Andy Hertzfeld (left). In 1979 Atkinson was an engineer working on Apple's ill-fated Lisa Project, when he convinced Steve Jobs to come with him to Xerox PARC to see the graphical operating system it had developed for the Alto computer. Jobs agreed, and told Xerox that he would allow the company to invest a million dollars in Apple if it would "open the kimono" for him – that is, give him a behind-the-scenes tour of PARC. When the kimono was opened Jobs was astounded by what he saw, and he told Atkinson to make the Lisa look like the Alto. Atkinson later moved to the Macintosh division of the company, where he developed MacPaint and HyperCard. Andy Hertzfeld developed most of the original system software for the Macintosh. Atkinson and Hertzfeld are shown here with Marc Porat in 1990; the three were founders of a technology company called General Magic.

NeXT

After losing his job at Apple in 1985, Steve Jobs founded NeXT Computer, which produced high-end personal computers and sophisticated software. He used US$7 million of his own money to start the company and hired a few key members of the Macintosh team to work for him. In 1987 Jobs had a factory built to make his computer, called the NeXTcube. Jobs's relentless perfectionism was at play at every level of the project, including aspects that weren't mission-critical: he was unhappy with the shade of grey used to paint the walls of the factory, so he had them repainted several times. When the NeXTcube was introduced in 1990, well behind schedule, people balked at its US$9,999 price. Only 50,000 NeXT computers were sold, but the machine has two claims to fame: World Wide Web inventor Tim Berners-Lee used a NeXT machine to develop the first Web server and browser and, in 1996, Apple bought NeXT for US$450 million and used the NeXT operating system as the basis for the new Macintosh operating system. As part of the deal, Jobs also returned to Apple as CEO.

⊢ Windows

In 1981 Steve Jobs showed Microsoft CEO Bill Gates an early version of what would become the Macintosh.

In 1983 Microsoft announced that it was going to develop a replacement for its command-line interface

software, DOS. The new operating system would be called Windows. When it was released in 1985, it was

roundly derided as clunky, slow, bug-ridden and useless. To make things worse, Apple filed a suit against

Microsoft for infringing the Macintosh's "look and feel". Windows 2, released in 1987, was better, and

Windows 3.0, released in 1990, made the platform a truly useful operating system. Today, Windows runs on

more than 90 per cent of personal computers.

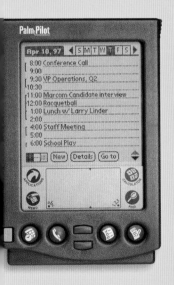  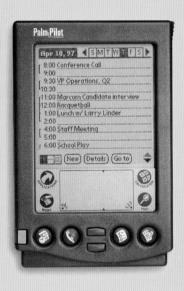 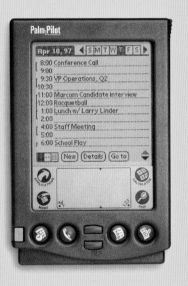 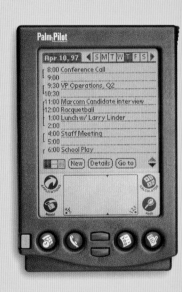

↑ Palm Pilot

While Jeff Hawkins was inventing the Palm Pilot handheld computer, he carried a block of wood the size of the Pilot in his pocket so he could get a feeling for what it would be like to carry around a personal digital assistant (PDA). When he was finished, in 1994, the small device became an icon of the mid-1990s. Unlike Apple's disastrous Newton handheld computer, the Palm Pilot was fast, had an excellent battery life and its handwriting recognition really worked. Microsoft soon got into the pocket PC game as well. It developed a version of Windows for handhelds and computer companies, such as Dell and Compaq, began making powerful handheld computers to run the system. Today, stand-alone handhelds are on the way out, because people prefer mobile phones.

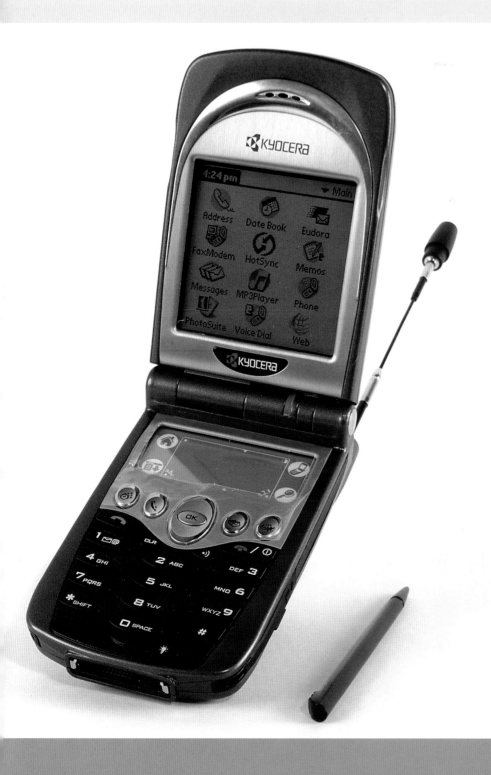

←| ←| ←| Smartphones

Will smartphones make personal computers a thing of the past? Probably not, but they'll certainly take over some of the chores now relegated to desktop and notebook computers. A smartphone is basically a personal digital assistant (PDA) combined with a mobile phone, usually featuring other functions such as a still or video camera, Internet access and email. Some smartphones can now receive television broadcasts and play MP3 files. Eventually, smartphones could become the conduit through which all our documents – letters, video clips, films – pass. The phone could be linked wirelessly to large screens, keyboards and mice, making it a combined phone, PDA and computer.

←| ←| Smart Personal Objects Technology

At the Las Vegas Comdex convention held in late 2002, Bill Gates unveiled Microsoft's Smart Personal Objects Technology (with its convenient acronym of SPOT). Gates explained that SPOT technology would allow "small devices, whether they're pocket-sized, or wrist-sized, tablet-sized, wallet-sized [to] come together". A SPOT wristwatch can display weather conditions, provide film listings and receive news updates. While SPOT has so far failed to win public acclaim, the idea of small objects communicating with the Internet and each other is sure to catch on eventually.

←| Tablet PC

As laptop computer components continue to shrink, it becomes easier to place them behind the flat panel monitor instead of under the keyboard. So, in certain instances, it makes sense to get rid of the keyboard altogether. What you're left with is a tablet PC – basically a notebook computer with a touch-screen. You can use a tablet PC to read online newspapers, watch films and take notes. Microsoft chairman Bill Gates is a tablet PC user. In 2001, he told Comdex attendees: "The PC took computing out of the back office and into everyone's office. The tablet takes cutting-edge PC technology and makes it available wherever you want it, which is why I'm already using a tablet as my everyday computer. It's a PC that is virtually without limits – and within five years I predict it will be the most popular form of PC sold in America."

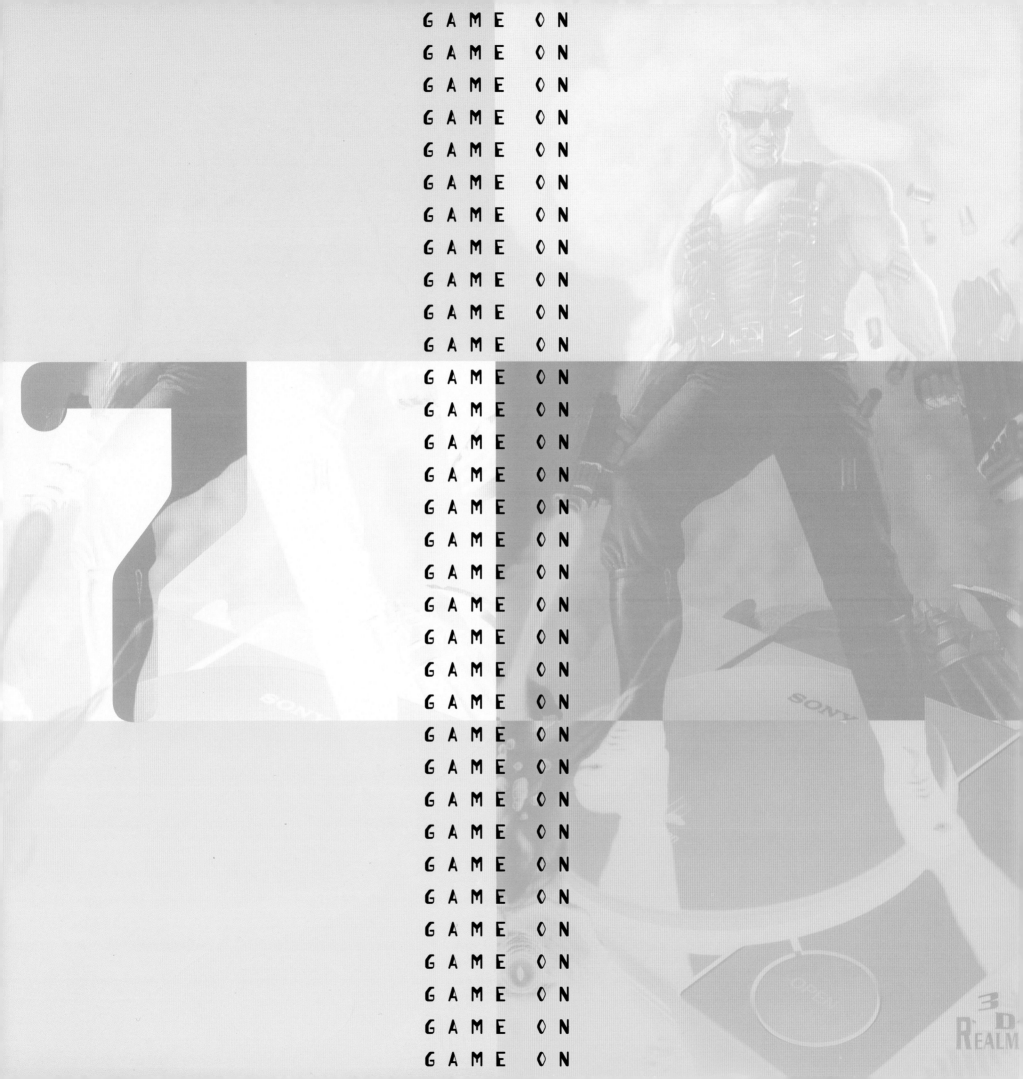

It's a well-known fact that video games generate far more money than films do. Video games are an essential part of millions of people's entertainment diet. They're here to stay.

But the unstoppable games industry wasn't always so stable. Consider the story of the rise and fall of Atari, a former giant in the games industry. In the late 1960s Nolan Bushnell was an electrical engineering student at the University of Utah. Like many other techie students at the time, Bushnell enjoyed playing an early computer game called Spacewar!, which ran on the university's mainframe computer. A few years after Bushnell graduated, he and a friend made a game that was closely inspired by Spacewar!, which he called Computer Space. Instead of running off an expensive mainframe computer, Computer Space was contained inside a stylish cabinet. He sold a few to pinball arcades, but the game proved to be too difficult to play and the venture was a flop.

At his next attempt, Bushnell decided to keep things simple. His game was called Pong, a ping-pong simulator that required nothing more of the player than to twiddle a knob to move an onscreen paddle and hit a ball. In 1972 he started a new company called Atari and started selling Pong to arcades and bars. This time, he had more luck – people loved the game. Unfortunately, though, a rash of Pong imitators rushed in and kept Pong from becoming a giant moneymaker for Atari.

In 1974 Atari made a home version of Pong and it was a hit. But other companies, such as Fairchild Semiconductor, were starting to move in with consoles that could play different games simply by inserting game cartridges into a slot. Atari didn't have enough capital to move fast enough to make a competing player, so Bushnell went looking for money. In 1976 Warner Communications bought Atari for US$28 million, after an executive at the company discovered that a US$4,500 Pong arcade game installed in a bar was generating US$250,000 a year, 25 cents at a time.

In 1977 the newly acquired company introduced the Atari 2600, a colour game console that sold for US$199 and had a slot to accept game cartridges. Atari sold 250,000 players that year, and 550,000 the following year. Unfortunately, it had manufactured 800,000 in 1978. The overstock put Atari in jeopardy. The troubles generated rancour between Bushnell and Warner management, and in 1978 Bushnell was out. But Warner stayed in. The company continued to develop new game titles, and in 1979 more than one million players were sold.

By 1980 Atari was making more for Warner than its record division. (Revenues for Atari were US$512 million, while the record division brought in US$446 million.) In 1981 Atari revenues surged again, this time to US$1.2 billion. Ten thousand people were working in Atari, up from 3,000 when it was purchased. For a time, Atari was the fastest-growing company in US history. They were the king of the hill, and Warner shareholders were overjoyed.

And then came the fall. It started with the release of Pac-Man in 1982, a wildly popular arcade game at the time. People couldn't get enough of the cute yellow pill-popping character, which uttered bleeps and blips as it ran through a maze populated by deadly goblins. Atari bet big on the success of Pac-Man and manufactured millions of cartridges to meet the expected demand. But the Atari home version was, by all accounts, a colossal dud. The animation was clunky and uneven, and the moribund sound effects were nothing like the chipper sounds that arcade players had grown accustomed to. Dissatisfied customers flocked to stores to return their copies.

Atari had even worse luck with E.T., a game based on the 1982 film *E.T. the Extra-Terrestrial*. Ray Kassar, the CEO of Atari at the time, purchased the rights from Steven Spielberg for an unprecedented US$20 million, an unbelievable amount of money for a game at that time. Atari also decided to manufacture five million E.T. cartridges, even though there were fewer than five million Atari 2600 players in existence.

Atari was in a rush to make the E.T. game available for the Christmas shopping season, and it gave its programmers just eight weeks to create the game from scratch. As you might expect, given the time constraints, it was horrendous. Players hated the plot, which involved collecting components to build a device that would allow E.T. to "phone home". Today, many 2600 collectors consider E.T. to be the worst video game ever made.

As a result of having two monumentally expensive failures on its books, Warner was forced to issue a press release on 9 December 1982, stating that Atari was experiencing "disappointing" sales. That day, Warner shares went into freefall. The company's value was cut by one-third. Shares plummeted from US$52 to US$35. A Warner executive in charge of overseeing Atari said he had been stunned as he watched "a business that disappeared in 20 minutes". In the days to follow, Warner's stock price continued to sink, hitting a low of US$7.

In September 1983 Warner Communications, stuck with millions of game cartridges that were so bad they couldn't give them away, loaded up 14 large trucks with E.T. and Pac-Man game cartridges, which had been kept in the company's El Paso, Texas warehouse. The trucks drove to Alamogordo, New Mexico, where the games were dumped into a landfill. It was probably unnecessary to crush the games by running over them with bulldozers – who would want to steal them? – but they crushed them anyway, along with any hopes of ever returning to the giddy boom days they had once experienced. Ten months later, Warner sold Atari to Jack Tramiel for US$240 million, a mere pittance compared to the damage Atari had cost the company.

Atari changed hands several times in the ensuing years but never managed to regain its lost lustre. In the end, the Atari name was sold to toymaker Hasbro for US$5 million. Had it not been for Pac-Man and E.T., who knows how much of today's annual US$10 billion video game pie would belong to Atari?

Contact

In 1933 The Pacific Amusements Co. in Los Angeles, California, introduced the first electromechanical pinball machine, called Contact. With yellow lightning bolts printed on the playing surface, it made all other pinball games obsolete. Before Contact, pinball machines relied entirely on gravity and the mechanical flippers to keep a ball moving. Contact used solenoids to send the ball careening across the field. It was also the first game to feature a ringing bell. In 1932 there were 150 companies making pinball machines. Before video games began to rule the arcades, pinball companies made more than 100,000 machines per year. Today, only one pinball machine maker exists, producing a scant 10,000 machines a year.

Tennis for two

In 1958 a scientist named William Higinbotham at the Brookhaven National Laboratories in Upton, New York, wired together an analogue computer and an oscilloscope to make one of the world's first video games: Tennis for Two. It was built as a fun demonstration for an open-house tour of Brookhaven National Laboratories, a nuclear research lab. The game depicted a long horizontal line (representing the tennis court) bisected by a short vertical line (the net). Higinbotham built two handheld controllers out of metal boxes, each with a knob and a button. The game was so popular that people waited for hours to have a turn at it. Higinbotham never tried to cash in on his invention, leaving it to entrepreneurs who would do that in the 1970s.

Spacewar!

Steve Russell, known to his pals as "Slug", was a member of the Tech Model Railroad Club at the Massachusetts Institute of Technology (MIT). When the university installed a Digital Equipment Corporation PDP-1 minicomputer in 1962, Slug and his fellow Model Railroad Club members decided to create a computer video game based on the novels of science fiction writer E E "Doc" Smith. They called their game Spacewar! and it pitted two spaceships against each other within a field of stars. The game featured realistic gravity and a clever hyperspace escape feature, which allowed a player to dodge a bullet by disappearing and reappearing at a random location on the screen. Like Higinbotham, Slug didn't think to patent or market his invention, which was brazenly copied in later years by companies who reaped great rewards from their games.

Periscope

In 1966 Sega made its first game – an electromechanical submarine combat arcade game called Periscope. At a time when pinball cost a dime (10 cents) to play in American games arcades, Periscope charged 25 cents per play. Nevertheless, the game was an astounding success. A promotional flyer for Periscope listed a number of innovative features not found in other arcade games at the time, such as realistic sound effects, explosion animations and a unique periscope interface.

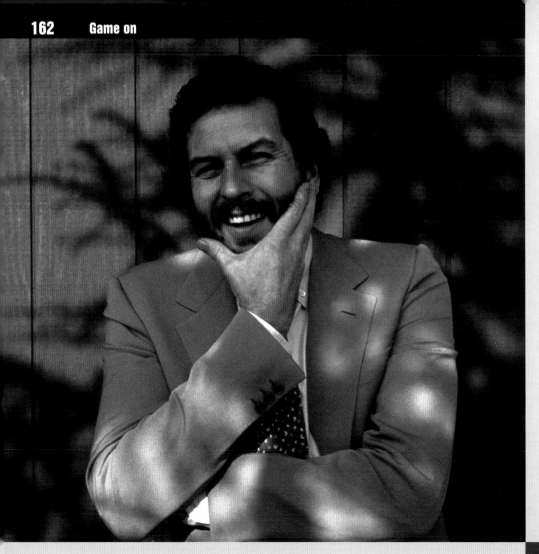

⟵ Nolan Bushnell

Most people think Pong was the first arcade video game but a year earlier, in 1971, Nutting Associates in Mountain View, California, released Computer Space, a brazen clone of the Spacewar! game that Steve Russell had developed at MIT in 1962. Computer Space was housed in a curvy plastic cabinet that resembled a piece of furniture out of *2001: A Space Odyssey*. The game wasn't a hit, mainly because arcade customers weren't accustomed to playing games with complex controls such as the ones that Computer Space used. Undaunted, the game's creator, Nolan Bushnell, formed another company, called Atari. In 1972 that company gave him the hit game he was looking for: Pong.

⟶ Hunt the Wumpus

Today's computer strategy and adventure games, with their photorealistic settings and crisp animation, have their roots in a relatively simple, but fun and challenging, early computer game called Hunt the Wumpus. Written in 1972 by Gregory Yob and published in *Creative Computing* magazine, the game's object was to navigate through a honeycomb of caves in search of an elusive but dangerous creature called the Wumpus. If you shot an arrow into a cave containing the Wumpus, you won the game. If you entered a cave with the Wumpus, you were eaten. You also had to watch out for deadly pits and giant bats that would pick you up and carry you off to a random cave. The game used no graphics – it was strictly a text adventure.

Another new game from Creative Computing....

HUNT THE WUMPUS

BY GREGORY YOB

The Genesis of Wumpus

Two years ago I happened by People's Computer Company (PCC) and saw some of their computer games — such as Hurkle, Snark, and Mugwump. My reaction was: "EECH!" Each of these games was based on a 10 x 10 grid in Cartesian co-ordinates and three of them was too much for me. I started to think along the lines of: "There has to be a hide and seek computer game without that (exp. deleted) grid!!" In fact, why not a topological computer game — Imagine a set of points connected in some way and the player moves about the set via the interconnections.

That afternoon in meditation the phrase "Hunt the Wumpus" arrived, and Wumpus was born. He's still a bit vague in physical detail as most dedicated Wumpus hunters know, but appearances are part of the game. (If you like, send me a picture of your version of a Wumpus. Perhaps friendly Dave, our editor, will publish the best one in *Creative Computing*.) The grid I chose was the vertices of a dodecahedron — simply because it's my favorite Platonic solid and once, ages ago, I made a kite shaped like one. The edges became the connecting tunnels between the caves which were the set of points for the game.

My basic idea at this time was for the player to approach the Wumpus, back off, and come up to him by going around the dodecahedron. To my knowledge, this has never happened ... most players adopt other strategies rather than this cold-blooded approach.

Anyway ... how to get the Wumpus! How about an arrow which could turn corners as it goes from room to room. Let the hunter tell the arrow where to go and let it fly. The shortest round trip without reversals is 5 caves — and thus the Crooked Arrow.

Hmmm ... How does one sense the Wumpus? It's dark in yonder cave, and light would wake him up. If one got one cave away, the wumpus's distinct smell would serve as a warning. So far, so good ... but Wumpus is still too easy, so let's find some appropriate hazards for the caves.

Bottomless pits were easy. Any imaginary cave would have a few of those around the place. Superbats were harder to come by. It took me a day or two to get that idea. The Superbats are a sort of rapid transit system gone a little batty (sorry about that one). They take you a random distance to a random cave and leave you there. If that's a pit or a Wumpus, well, you are in Fate's hands.

Around this time, I saw that Map-making would be a regular activity of Wumpus hunters. I numbered the caves and made the scheme fixed in the hopes a practised player might notice this and make himself a permanent map of the caverns. (Another unrealised hope — as an exercise, make yourself such a map on a Squashed Dodecahedron).

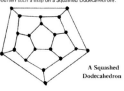

A Squashed Dodecahedron

To start the game fairly, Wumpus, Hazards, and Hunter are located on different points at the start of the game. Each game starts with random choices of location, but the hunter may restart with the same set-up if he chooses. This allows re-plays if the hunter, say, fell into a pit on the first move.

Wumpus was nearly done in my mind... (hint to a games-writer: Have a clear notion of your game before you

Odyssey

On 27 January 1972 Magnavox introduced the first video game system for home use: the Odyssey Home Entertainment System. The primitive "ball and paddle" game system was designed by Ralph Baer, who was a consumer product development manager at a military electronics consulting firm called Sanders Associates. Baer based his invention on Higinbotham's Tennis for Two game but, unlike Higinbotham, Baer applied for a patent on his invention, which he called a "Television Gaming Apparatus". Magnavox licensed the technology from Baer and started selling the unit for US$100 through its chain of retail television stores. Unscrupulous dealers lied to would-be customers by telling them that the Odyssey would work only with Magnavox TV sets. This hurt the sales of the Odyssey, but Magnavox still managed to sell about 80,000 units that year. The Odyssey 100 replaced it in 1975.

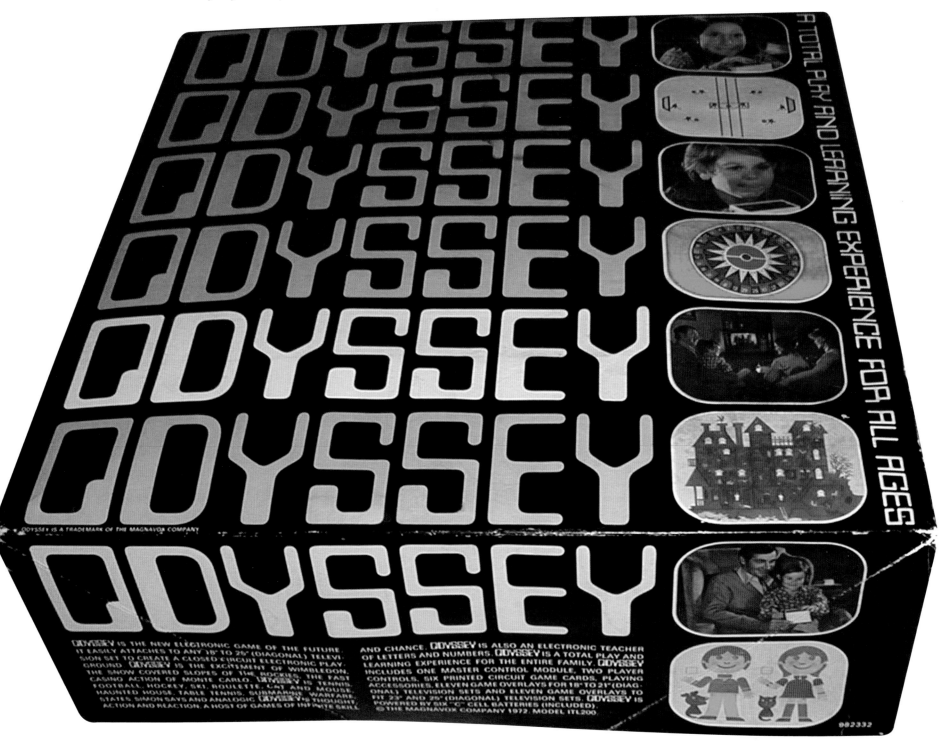

↑ ↦ Atari VSC/2600

In 1977 Atari introduced the VCS (Video Computer System) game console, which was later renamed the 2600. It was phenomenally successful and many adults have fond memories of it as their first gaming system. Selling for US$199, the 2600 had colour graphics, and consumers could buy nine different games, including Breakout and Pong. By 1979 Atari was selling one million units per year. In 1980 Atari posted a US$2 billion profit. By 1982 close to eight million Atari 2600 systems had been sold. But in 1983 Atari faced a drastic reversal when two of its most highly anticipated titles, Pac-Man and E.T., turned out to be flops. Warner Communications, which had purchased Atari from founder Nolan Bushnell in 1976 for US$28 million, sold the company in 1984 to Commodore. Atari never fully recovered. However, to this day, a legion of diehard Atari 2600 fanatics continue to develop new game titles for the system, and 2600 emulators are available for home computers.

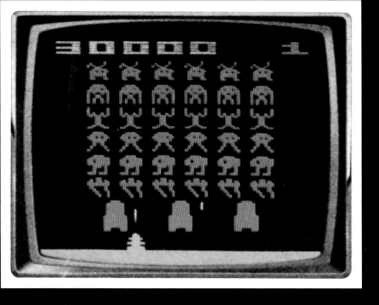

Space Invaders   Pong may have been the first video game to capture the public's attention, but Space

Invaders, introduced in 1978, was the first to capture the public's heart – and spare change. Designed by

Toshihiro Nishikado, the game is as elegantly simple as it is brilliant: rows and columns of menacing aliens

scroll across the sky and drop bombs, while you shoot them out of the sky with a cannon and unlimited

ammunition. The primitive graphics are greatly enhanced with what many gamers consider the finest video

game soundtrack ever written: a simple heartbeat, which becomes more urgent as the invaders descend and

threaten to overtake your planet. Space Invaders ruled Planet Earth (or at least the teenaged component) unt

1980, when a little yellow guy named Pac-Man arrived on the scene and knocked the game from its throne.

THE EXPLOSIVE ARCADE HIT!

BATTLEZONE™

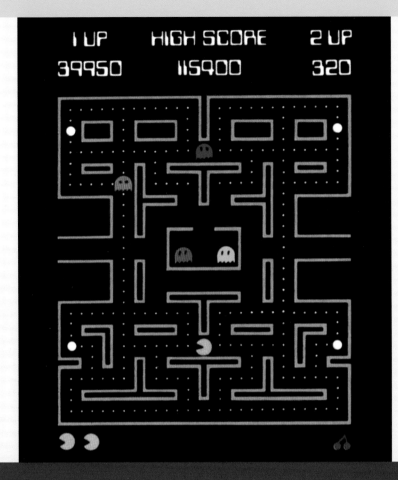

Pac-Man

Toru Iwatani was 25 years old when he invented Pac-Man for Namco Ltd, a Japanese software company. Self-trained as a programmer and unschooled in art or graphic design, Iwatani managed to create one of the most enduring and lucrative character franchises of the twentieth century. He says he came up with the character after eating a slice of a pizza he'd ordered for lunch and noticing the shape of the remaining pizza with the missing wedge. Pac-Man appeared in arcades in 1980 to great fanfare. The game features a little pill-eating circle that must run through a maze while avoiding hungry ghosts. In Japan it was called Puck Man – a play on the Japanese word pakupaku, an onomatopoeic term for the sound made when you rapidly open and close your mouth – but marketers wisely changed the game's name in markets outside Japan. They didn't want teenagers to vandalize the title of the game by changing the "P" to an "F".

Battlezone

In 1980 Atari's Battlezone took arcade video gaming into a new dimension – the third dimension. Battlezone was the first 3D, first-person perspective game, drawing tanks on the screen as simple 3D wireframes. By today's standards, Battlezone looks half-finished, but at the time it was state-of-the-art in video gaming terms. The port-hole window and dual-stick control system added a great deal to the fun of the game. Your assignment was to blow up as many enemy tanks as possible before they blew you up. The US Army was so impressed by the arcade game that it ordered Atari to build a special version to be used as a target gunner training system.

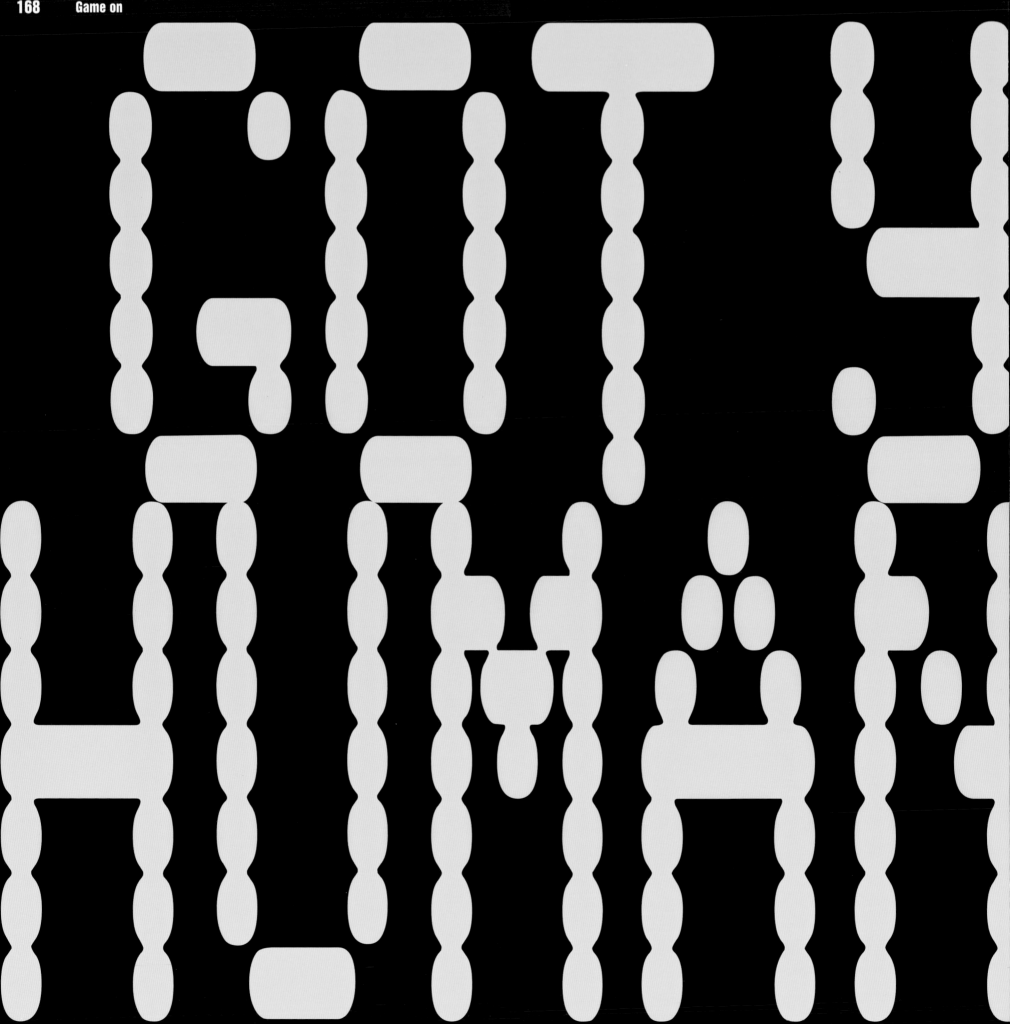

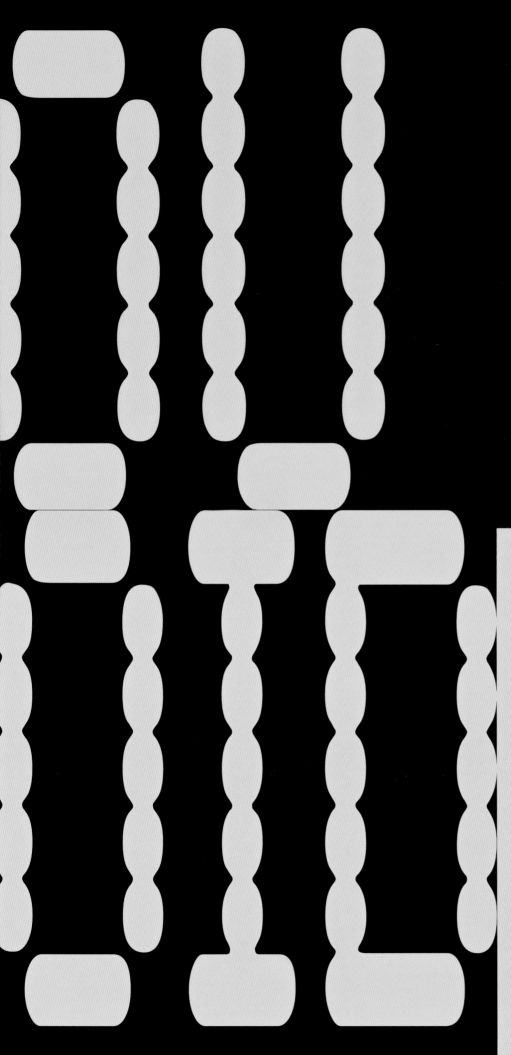

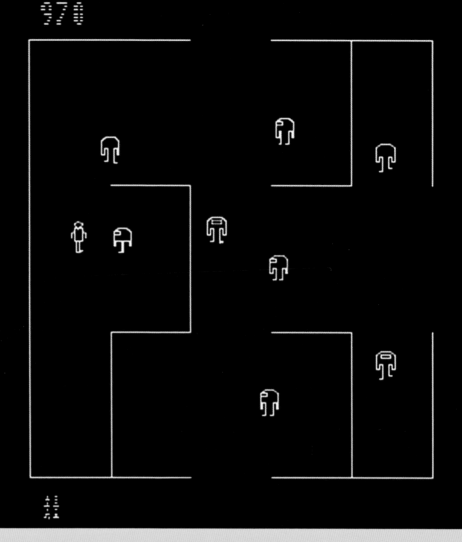

Berzerk

The first person to die from playing a video game was 19-year-old Jeff Dailey, who suffered

a massive heart attack after playing Berzerk in January 1981. Naturally, this made the

game even more popular. In Berzerk players control a human trapped in a deadly maze

populated with killer robots. If the character touches a wall or a robot, he dies. The game

also has one of the creepiest villains of all time – a smiley-faced circle named Evil Otto,

who is impervious to bullets and can penetrate walls. Berzerk was the first video game to

feature digitized speech and the robots were fond of saying: "Stop the Humanoid!"

Berzerk's distinction of being a dangerous game was hammered home in 1982, when it

claimed another human victim – an 18-year-old named Peter Burkowski, who, like Dailey,

died of a heart attack after playing the game.

← Shigeru Miyamoto

Donkey Kong creator Shigeru Miyamoto is the superstar of the video game world. He grew up without a TV set and spent most of his childhood exploring the environs of his rural upbringing in Japan. In 1977, then 24 years old, he went to work as an artist for Nintendo, which was still a non video game company. In 1980 his boss at Nintendo asked him to design a video game. Miyamoto presented him with Donkey Kong in 1983 and it was a giant hit. He then used the lead character from Donkey Kong, a stereotypical little Italian fellow named Mario, in Super Mario Brothers in 1985. In addition to producing and/or directing other hit titles for Nintendo, such as The Legend of Zelda, Miyamoto is credited with inventing the analogue controller and the "left right" buttons. Today, he's the director and general manager of Nintendo entertainment analysis and development.

Tetris

Alexey Pajitnov was working at the Russian Academy of Sciences in Moscow as an artificial intelligence researcher when he invented Tetris in 1985. The game is deceptively simple, but extremely addictive. The object is to rotate different-shaped blocks as they fall from the sky so that they land in rows. When a row is filled with blocks, it disappears. Once the blocks reach the top of the screen, you lose. When the game appeared in arcades, on personal computers and in home video games, people reported having dreams about Tetris and comparing everyday activities, such as changing lanes while driving, to the game. Nintendo sold 35 million copies of Tetris on the GameBoy alone. Unfortunately, owing to the many unauthorized Tetris clones and unlicensed versions floating around, Pajitnov made very little money from his smash hit.

Nintendo Entertainment System

The great video game crash of 1983 was still in effect when the NES (Nintendo Entertainment System) hit store shelves in 1985. Fortunately for the industry, though, it was an instant winner, thanks in no small part to the thrilling Super Mario Brothers game designed for the system by Nintendo game legend Shigeru Miyamoto. With excellent graphics and sound (for the time), more than 60 million NES units were sold around the world. In 1990 Nintendo knocked Toyota out of the top spot as the most profitable company in Japan.

Sega Master System

The Sega Master System was introduced in Japan in October 1985 and the USA in June 1985. Although it had better graphics than the NES, it was not as successful as the Nintendo game console. For one thing, Nintendo had beaten Sega to the market. For another, Nintendo had Shigeru Miyamoto and Sega didn't. (Apparently, Sega's most popular character, Sonic the Hedgehog, was no match against Mario.) While the SMS sold rather poorly in the USA and Japan, it did well in South America and a version of the game console is still produced in Brazil.

Atari 7800

The Atari 5200, released in 1982, was a flop. Even
though it was cheaper and better in many respects than
competing systems (made by Coleco and Mattel), it
suffered from three problems: a lousy joystick;
incompatibility with the huge library of Atari 2600
games that many people still wanted to play; and a
depressed video game market. Atari attempted to
remedy the situation in 1984 with the release of the
7800, which was compatible with 2600 games and
featured a better joystick. The 7800 could also be
easily converted into a functional personal computer,
with the purchase of a keyboard and plug-in
peripherals. The 7800 was never a big success,
however, because the company didn't offer good
support to the game developer community, which
resulted in a dearth of titles for the machine. The 7800
proved another nail in the coffin for the Atari brand.

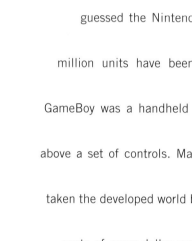

Nintendo GameBoy

What's the best-selling video game player ever? If you

guessed the Nintendo GameBoy, give yourself a pat on the back – 168

million units have been sold since it was introduced in 1989. The original

GameBoy was a handheld game player that sported a small black-and-green screen

above a set of controls. Many people bought GameBoys just to play Tetris, which had

taken the developed world by storm. Today, GameBoy players and games represent "25

cents of every dollar spent in the North American industry", boasts a Nintendo

spokesperson. The latest GameBoy model is far more advanced than the

original, featuring two illuminated colour screens and

wireless connectivity.

Trip Hawkins

In 1982 Trip Hawkins was heading up the strategy and marketing division for Apple Computer when he quit his job to form a video game company called Electronic Arts. With an eye for detail and excellent gameplay, the company quickly grabbed an enormous share of the market. (Today, it's the biggest games publishing company in the world.) Hawkins tried to repeat his success in 1991 when he launched another video game company called 3DO. His idea was to develop a video game console and then license the design to other companies, which would manufacture the players and pay 3DO a royalty. But the first 3DO player on the market, introduced in 1993, cost a staggering US$700. Even though it was a sophisticated machine, customers balked. For the next decade, 3DO limped along developing video game titles, but it never got the hit it needed to break into the big leagues. 3DO went out of business in 2003. Today, Hawkins is working at his latest start-up, a mobile phone game company called Digital Chocolate.

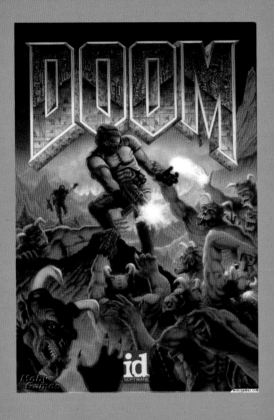

Doom

For better or worse, Doom changed the nature of video games. When it was released by id Software in 1995, the media praised its innovative "first-person shooter" interface, user customizability and its capability for rendering graphics at lightning speed. Others decried its excessively gory violence. The plot of the game concerns a lone military special forces soldier (controlled by the player) battling demons from hell that are pouring through the gates of a teleportation system between the moons of Mars. As the game progresses, the player's character can resort to a variety of increasingly deadly weapons, including the BFG9000 (you can probably guess what "BFG" stands for). As many as 20 million people downloaded the shareware version of Doom and 1.5 million paid for the full version.

Sega Saturn

In 1995 Sega wanted to get its 32-bit games console, the Saturn, on to store shelves before Sony introduced its PlayStation. Sega beat Sony by a few weeks, but because it rushed, Sega didn't have many games available for the unit. The machine was also difficult to write games for. Programmers had a hard time figuring out how to make the best use of the Saturn's eight different processors, including two central processing units. Many programmers wrote games that utilized just a single CPU, effectively halving the machine's power. Another problem with the Saturn was its price. It cost US$400, while the PlayStation cost US$300. Compared to the PlayStation and Nintendo 64, the Saturn was a flop.

Sony PlayStation

Sony's PlayStation, introduced in 1995, is one of the best-selling consoles in the world. More than 100 million units and 950 million games have been sold. Sony took the innovative step of using CDs for the games' medium – they were cheaper and more capacious than cartridges. Sony also offered a library of titles that appealed to older teens and adults, which helped spur sales. In 1996 the PlayStation's price dropped to US$199. But the PlayStation didn't really take off until the release of Final Fantasy VII in 1997. The game was so popular that many people bought PlayStations just so they could play it.

Nintendo 64

Nintendo 64, released on 29 September 1996, was the last of the cartridge-playing games.

(Everyone else had switched over to cheaper CDs.) For Nintendo, it was a smart move –

cartridges can transfer data much more quickly than a CD and the unit's 64-bit chip was plenty

fast enough to handle the data. Nintendo also went against the grain by selling the unit

(US$199) without an accompanying game. Nevertheless, 500,000 units were sold the day it

went on sale. Most people bought Super Mario 64, one of only two titles available at launch. No

matter – the 3D world of Super Mario 64 was so engaging that it was hailed "the greatest video

game ever made" by *Next Generation* magazine.

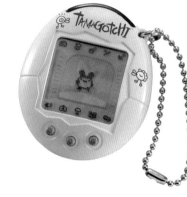

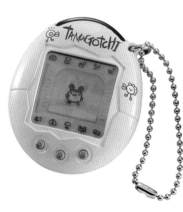
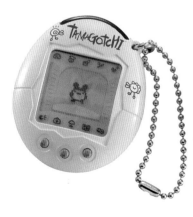
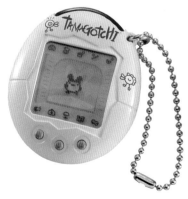
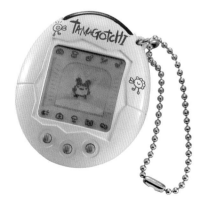

Tamagotchi

Computer games weren't just relegated to consoles and computers. In 1996 Japanese company Bandai introduced Tamagotchi, a handheld virtual pet. Housed in a little plastic egg containing a liquid crystal display monitor and a couple of buttons, the tiny cartoon creature demanded to be fed and played with. Owners also had to clean up after their pet, care for it when it was ill and discipline it when it misbehaved. If owners didn't pay attention to the Tamagotchi, it would die – and they'd have to start over. Forty million Tamagotchis were sold worldwide. But Bandai, anticipating an ever-growing market, miscalculated the demand and made too many of the toys. In the end, the company ended up losing about six billion yen on Tamogotchi.

Deep Blue

Computer games took a more serious turn in 1997 when Garry Kasparov, the chess champion of the world, was bested by a computer – IBM's Deep Blue. (The name pays homage to the Deep Thought computer from *The Hitchhiker's Guide to the Galaxy* novels by Douglas Adams.) It wasn't the first time the two master players had met. In 1996 Kasparov won the tournament with a score of 4–2. IBM went back to the lab and reprogrammed Deep Blue: the computer won the rematch with a score of 3.5–2.5. Some might say the computer had an unfair advantage. Deep Blue had almost 500 specially designed processors dedicated to analyzing the outcomes of every possible move, while its human opponent had to rely on just one processor – his brain.

Xbox

Microsoft entered the computer games arena in November 2001 with the Xbox console. Instead of using a proprietary design for the machine, the company went with what it knew best and used PC components. It also put a hard drive in the Xbox, which meant players didn't need to buy flash memory cards to save game scores. Microsoft knew it was entering a tough market when it chose to go head to head with Sony and Nintendo. The company predicted it wouldn't turn a profit on the Xbox for three years and by 2005 it still hadn't. So far, the Xbox division – the largest division in the company – has lost more than $1 billion. Nevertheless, the Xbox has some of the most popular titles in gaming, including Halo 2.

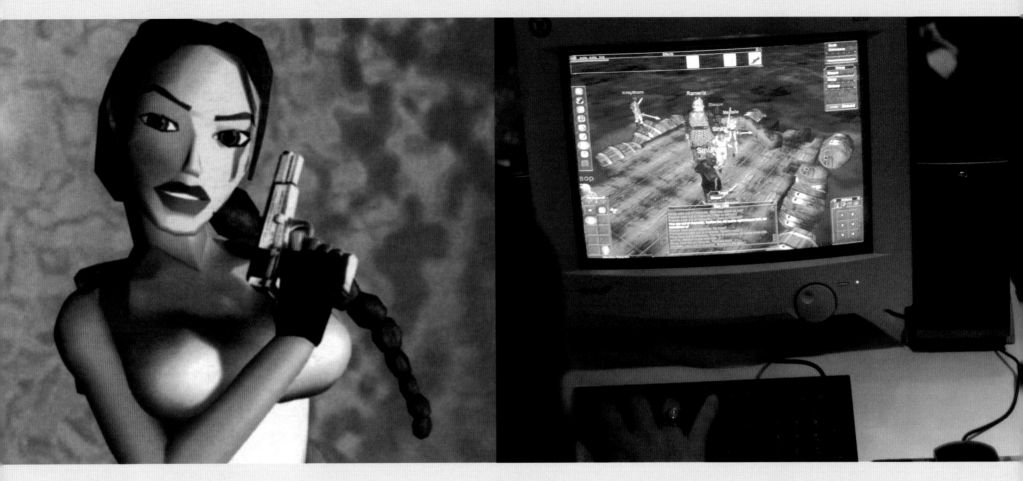

Tomb Raider

Toby Gard took a chance when he cast a female in the lead role for the video game Tomb Raider, but it paid off. Lara Croft has turned out to be one of the most popular characters to emerge from a video game. The sexy adventuress (said to have been born in England in 1968) works as a freelance "tomb raider" – that is, she sneaks into archaeological sites and recovers lost and stolen treasures. In 2001 Lara Croft hit the big screen in a film version of Tomb Raider starring Angelina Jolie.

EverQuest

With almost 500,000 people playing it, EverQuest is one of the most popular massively multiplayer online role-playing games (MMORPG). Players pay a monthly fee to enter an online fantasy world of witchcraft and warcraft, battling monsters and forming alliances with other players. Players can assume the guises of different human and non-human characters, such as elves or trolls, and join guilds to help complete complex quests for treasure as well as powerful artifacts and weapons. Since the launch of EverQuest in 1999, many other MMORPGs have been introduced, the most popular being in South Korea, where millions of people play Nexus: The Kingdom of the Winds, Lineage and Ragnarok Online.

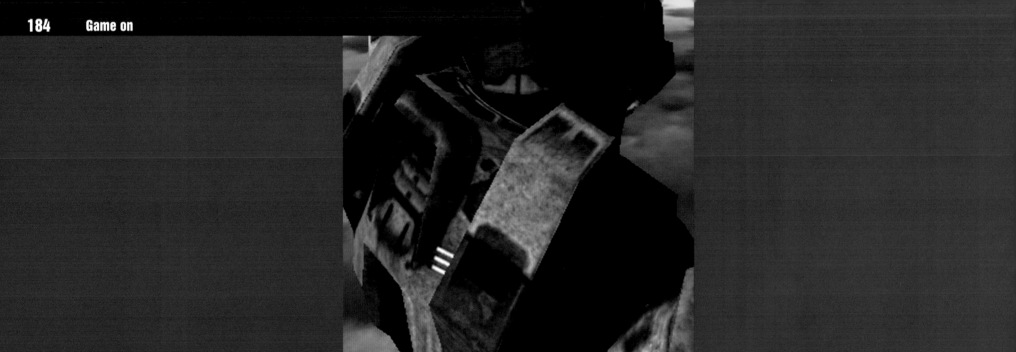

Halo 2

The best-selling Xbox game Halo 2 (2004) immerses players in a cinematic adventure by using advanced artificial intelligence, physics simulation destructible environments, realistic lighting and high-fidelity sound effects. Halo's maker, Bungie, was launched in 1991 with the release of a Pong clone called Gnop. Bungie then released two games for the Macintosh: Operation Desert Storm and Minotaur, each of which sold just 2,500 copies. Compare that with Halo 2, which sold 2.4 million copies on the day it was released, for a total of US$125 million.

JACKING IN

JACKING IN

JACKING IN

JACKING IN

JACKING IN

JACKING IN

JACKING IN

JACKING IN

JACKING IN

JACKING IN

JACKING IN

JACKING IN

JACKING IN

JACKING IN

JACKING IN

JACKING IN

JACKING IN

JACKING IN

JACKING IN

JACKING IN

JACKING IN

JACKING IN

JACKING IN

JACKING IN

JACKING IN

JACKING IN

JACKING IN

JACKING IN

JACKING IN

JACKING IN

Sometimes, it's hard to remember what life was like before the Web. Back in the pre-Web days, if you had a question (How long should you boil a potato for? What's a good place to take an island vacation? How does one install a rain gutter? What's the most effective treatment for mesothelioma?) you'd call a friend, visit the local library or hire an expert.

Today, more than 100 million people, ask Google, the number one search engine on the Web. Google has become the ready-reference guide to the world, collecting data from billions of Web pages and indexing them in such a way that it takes just a fraction of a second to search through the largest repository of data the world has ever known. If the adage "information is power" is true, then Google has given each of us the equivalent of a 100-megawatt nuclear reactor.

Even though Google is a free service, the company has made its young founders, Larry Page and Sergey Brin, billionaires. (The company makes money through advertising and by licensing its search technology to corporations.) But without the Web, from which Google draws its value, Page and Brin might be just another couple of engineers toiling away in a cubicle somewhere. They owe a great deal of thanks to the man who invented the World Wide Web, Tim Berners-Lee. Like Page and Brin, Berners-Lee gave his creation to the world. But unlike the Google founders, Berners-Lee never sought to make money from his invention. (Does that make him nobler? Who's to say? He does have a noble title, however: in 2004 the Queen made him a Knight Commander in the Order of the British Empire.)

People often confuse the Web and the Internet, using the words interchangeably. But there's a difference. The Internet is the network of interconnected computer networks that use a standard method of exchanging data, while the Web is a kind of service that uses the Internet. Before the Web came along, the Internet wasn't a very user-friendly place (with the exception of email). There was no point-and-click way to exchange information with other people. Searching was almost non-existent – in order to find something, you had to know where to look for it.

Tim Berners-Lee thought there was room for improvement. Born in London and educated at Oxford, Berners-Lee knew a lot about computers. In fact, his parents were both mathematicians who had programmed the world's first commercial computer, the Ferranti Mark I. When Berners-Lee was still at high school, he had a conversation with his father about the human brain's wonderful ability to make non-obvious relationships between different concepts, something computers couldn't do.

This idea never left Berners-Lee, even years later when, in 1980, he went to work at CERN, the European Particle Physics Laboratory in Switzerland. One of his projects was to develop a system that kept track of the people who were responsible for the many different research efforts underway at the laboratory. His system used "hypertext", which linked certain words in the text of the online documents to other documents. Today, we all use hypertext on the Web and don't think of it as an extraordinary thing, but 25 years ago it was revolutionary stuff. Berners-Lee named his programme Enquire, after a favourite Victorian book his family owned when he was a child, called *Enquire Within upon Everything*.

Berners-Lee left CERN in 1981 to work on computer graphics but returned in 1984, determined to secure funding for a full-blown hypertext initiative. He proposed an international hypertext system, one that would allow high-energy physicists around the world to exchange documents instantaneously with the click of a key. It wasn't until 1990 that he developed the world's first Web browser (which he called WorldWideWeb), on a NeXT computer. Berners-Lee realized that one of the key aspects of the Web would be its editability – all Web users should have the tools to create and modify pages and make them accessible to all other Web users.

On 6 August 1991 Berners-Lee posted a message to a hypertext discussion group on the Internet announcing the availability of his invention: "The World-WideWeb (WWW) project aims to allow links to be made to any information anywhere," he wrote. At the time, only the nascent community of hypertext researchers was interested in WWW. But on 30 April 1993 Berners-Lee did something that would ensure the success of the Web: he convinced the higher-ups at CERN to release the World Wide Web to the public domain, allowing anyone to use it and modify it to their heart's content. And use it they did. After other people started creating easy-to-use browsers, such as Mosaic – written by a 23-year-old University of Illinois graduate named Marc Andreessen – and giving them away in 1993, the Web exploded.

At that time, in January 1993, there were 50 known Web servers. By October there were more than 500. By June 1994 there were 1,500. Today, there are millions. The fact that the Web operates so well today, even though it is many orders of magnitude larger than even Berners-Lee himself ever dreamed, is testament to his genius.

In a few short years, the Web went from being an obscure research project at a Swiss laboratory that hardly anyone had heard of, to being the fastest-growing form of media the world had ever known. And most people would agree that we're still in the early stages of the Web. As Internet connections get faster, it's not hard to imagine that the Web will subsume television and radio, because the Web can offer what both of these old forms of media offer, plus give users the ability to record, schedule and search for content.

Tim Berners-Lee isn't finished with the Web, either. In fact, he believes his work has just begun. From his offices at the World Wide Web Consortium in Cambridge, Massachusetts, Berners-Lee is leading the development of a major project he calls the Semantic Web. The goal is to create a new version of the Web in which information can be used by computers to form novel associations between different pieces of information on the Net. If that happens, then it really will be possible to enquire within upon everything. With the help of Google, of course.

Leonard Kleinrock

Packet-switching is the thing that makes the Internet special. It represents a radical departure from other electronic networks, such as the phone companies', which use circuit-switched connections. When you make a phone call, a phone company establishes a dedicated connection between you and the person you're calling. But when you send an email message or view a web page, the Internet breaks your message into discrete packets and routes them from computer to computer, with no set connection. There is some controversy as to who actually invented packet-switching. Some credit computer scientist Leonard Kleinrock (shown here), while others say it was invented by Paul Baran and Donald Davies in 1962.

Ray Tomlinson

Email is truly the "killer app" (application) of the Internet. Each year, the citizens of the world send trillions of email messages to each other. Have you ever wondered who came up with the idea for using the "@" symbol to separate user names from domains in email addresses? You can stop wondering: it was programmer Ray Tomlinson (b 1941), who came up with it in 1971. While Tomlinson's convention and programmes helped establish email as a means of communication, he didn't invent email. The first email messages were sent in 1965 between users of large university mainframe computers. When computers became networked shortly thereafter, email was used to send messages between users of different systems.

John Draper

Before the Internet, there were phreakers – people who hacked into the phone system. John

Draper was the most notorious. In the early 1970s he got the nickname Captain Crunch

because he had learned how to use a toy whistle, found in boxes of Cap'n Crunch breakfast

cereal, to create tones that would give him special access to phone networks. He was arrested

for his mischievous deeds in 1972 and got five years' probation. A few years later, he taught

Steve Jobs and Steve Wozniak how to make devices called "blue boxes" that would enable

people to make free phone calls. When Jobs and Wozniak later formed Apple, they hired Draper

to work for them, but Draper was again arrested, this time for wire fraud, in 1977. Today, he

works as a computer security programmer.

Minitel

France was a step ahead of the rest of the world when it launched the Minitel network in 1982. The online computer service offered many things that today's Web offers: shopping, travel information and reservations, financial data, instant messaging and, yes, pornography. By 1999 25 million people were using Minitel. When the Web exploded around the rest of the world, Minitel began offering its services over the Web.

├─→ WarGames

The movie *WarGames* (1983) introduced the film-going public to the hacker – typically,

a young man with a personal computer, modem and the skills needed to penetrate

secure networks. In the movie, Matthew Broderick plays a high school student who

uses his home computer to stumble into a top-secret military computer system, which

contains an artificial intelligence programme that controls the USA's nuclear arsenal.

Broderick mistakenly thinks he has cracked into a games company and proceeds to

goad the artificial intelligence into preparing to launch a massive nuclear strike against

the Soviets. While the movie was loaded with technical errors, it also inspired

thousands of teenagers to get involved with online computing.

├─→ Stewart Brand

After riding around on Ken Kesey's bus during the Acid Tests of the psychedelic Sixties, Stewart Brand started selling buttons that read:

"Why Haven't We Seen A Photograph of the Whole Earth Yet?" This was in 1966. Two years later, when NASA finally did photograph the

Earth from space, Brand put the picture on the cover of his book, *The Whole Earth Catalog*, an alternative living publication that sold

1.5 million copies. From early on, Brand was interested in computers as tools for individuals, and in 1984, he founded The WELL (Whole

Earth 'Lectronic Link), a pre-Web computer bulletin board that became a famous hang-out for early online enthusiasts.

Mondo 2000

Mondo 2000, a "cyberculture" magazine founded in 1989, celebrated the strange links between psychedelic drugs, sex, music and computers. Editors R U Sirius and Queen Mu delighted in virtual reality, cybersex, hacking, artificial life and music sampling. As an early advocate of digital art and image manipulation, *Mondo 2000*'s art director, Bart Nagel, offered a fresh, startling vision for magazine design that was often imitated. Many of *Mondo 2000*'s contributors subsequently went on to work in Internet-related start-up companies.

Future Sex

Future Sex magazine, published in San Francisco during the early 1990s dotcom craze, attempted to mesh together two seemingly disparate topics: sex and computers. At the time, the idea of teledildonics (using virtual reality technology to have sex with another person remotely) was in vogue, though no one had really invented or marketed any equipment that even remotely matched up to the fantasy. Even so, *Future Sex* editor Lisa Palac was so frequently hit with requests by mainstream publications asking her to tell them where they could find examples of cybersex that she finally started telling the callers: "We made it all up."

$\longmapsto$ **GURPS Cyberpunk**

When Steve Jackson Games of Austin, Texas, published a role-playing game manual called *GURPS Cyberpunk*, in 1990, the offices were raided by armed agents of the US Secret Service. The agents seized a large number of computers and equipment from the company. The agents' justification: that the game was "a handbook for computer crime". If the agents had simply taken the time to sit down and read the manual, they would have quickly realized that GURPS Cyberpunk was exactly what its publisher claimed it was: a game. Eventually, Steve Jackson Games got its computers back, but only after a lot of legal wrangling. As a result of the fracas, civil libertarians in the USA started a cyber-rights organization, called the Electronic Frontier Foundation, to prevent such mishaps from occurring in the future.

World Wide Web

In the late 1980s Tim Berners-Lee was working as a programmer at CERN, the European Particle Physics Laboratory. One of the things he developed there was a system by which researchers at different research institutions around the world could easily exchange text and graphics using the Internet. In 1990 he unveiled his programme, calling it the World Wide Web. Berners-Lee (now Sir Tim Berners-Lee, after being knighted in 2004 for his invention) never sought a patent for his world-changing creation, preferring instead to give it to people to do whatever they wished with it. The picture shown is Berners-Lee's original Web browser programme.

Robert Morris

On 2 November 1988 Robert Morris, a computer science student at Cornell University, released on to the Internet a special kind of computer programme, called a worm, which could propagate from one computer to another, making copies of itself. Morris was not acting maliciously – he was merely curious to see where his worm would travel on the Net. However, the programme contained an error that made it replicate much more quickly than he expected and, as a result, the worm bogged down a great number of computers, including ones used by military and medical researchers. The worm took hundreds of man hours and hundreds of thousands of dollars to fix, and was one of the early indicators of the vulnerability of the Internet and the troubles that lay ahead. Morris was subsequently sentenced to three years' probation for violating the Computer Fraud and Abuse Act.

Linux

When it comes to computer operating systems, Microsoft may have more than 90 per cent of the computer users, but Linux has most of the smartest. This cost-free operating system, based on Unix (which was developed in the 1960s at AT&T Bell Labs) was developed by volunteers, led by Helsinki-born engineer Linus Torvalds. First released on the Internet in September 1991, Linux is a very popular operating system with hardcore computer nerds and its "open source" method of software development is now used to create thousands of other free software projects. When asked to comment on Linux, Microsoft CEO Steve Ballmer said the system is "one of the five problems which employ me before falling asleep. But I sleep nevertheless still quite well."

WIRED

Sep/Oct 1993

串連

William

His latest report

Gibson

from the future

Disneyland with the

isn't fiction

Death Penalty

George Gilder
The Dark Fiber Interview

Michael Crichton
The Real Dinosaurs are
the Media Special Fiction Bonus

Paulina Borsook
Love Over the Wires

$4.05 / Canada 5.95

←⊣ Wired

In the early 1990s a pair of Americans named Louis Rossetto and Jane Metcalfe, who had been living in Amsterdam, moved back to the USA and set up shop in a grimy office in San Francisco with plans to launch a general interest magazine about the digitization of information. The first issue of their magazine, which they called *Wired*, hit the stands in March 1993. It was accompanied by a bold proclamation from editor Rossetto: "The Digital Revolution is whipping through our lives like a Bengali typhoon." Oddly enough, the first issue of the magazine had no mention of the Internet. But that soon changed. *Wired* was one of the first magazines to have a website, HotWired, launched in October 1994, at a time when most people had never heard of the Web or the Internet. Today, *Wired* is read by more than 600,000 people.

Kevin Mitnick

The world's most notorious hacker, Kevin Mitnick, has an impressive rap sheet. In 1981, at the age of 18, he was convicted for breaking into phone companies, and in 1983 he was convicted for penetrating the security system of a Pentagon computer. He went into hiding for a number of years but continued to wreak havoc (he thought he was having harmless fun – most of the time, at least) on computer networks. When he was arrested in 1988, the fifth time he'd been apprehended for computer crimes, he pleaded guilty and went to prison, taking therapy to cure himself of his "addiction" to hacking. Today, he runs Mitnick Security Consulting and offers his services to companies that want to secure their networks against hackers.

Google

Using Google to search for something on the World Wide Web is so commonplace that "to Google" has become a part of the vernacular. The company was started as a research project in 1986 by two Stanford University grad students, Sergey Brin and Larry Page. At the time, most search engines, such as Alta Vista, didn't rank search results according to popularity or importance, and search directories, like Yahoo, used expensive human editors to find the most relevant websites for given keywords. Google's approach was an automated scouring of the Web to find out which sites other sites were linking to. Brin and Page developed an automated way to rank websites based on popularity, and as a result, Google has become the most-used search engine in the world, with more than 80 million monthly users worldwide.

1999
Jeff Bezos

Jeff Bezos

Who would have thought that a new medium, like the Web, would end up being one of the best ways to sell an old medium: books? A lot of people questioned Jeff Bezos's business savvy when he went on the road to drum up investors for an electronic shopping venture he was proposing, called Cadrabra.com. When it launched in 1994, few companies were selling products over the Internet (but other online services, such as Minitel and Prodigy, had been doing so for a decade). In 1995 Bezos changed the name to Amazon.com. When the company went public in 1997, Bezos told investors not to expect a profit for four years. It was a wise move, because when other dotcom businesses went bankrupt during the dot bomb collapse of 2000, Amazon managed to stay afloat. True to Bezos's word, in January 2004, Amazon announced its first profitable year – US$35 million, with revenues of US$5.65 billion.

Pierre Omidyar

In 1995 computer scientist Pierre Omidyar's girlfriend asked him if he could come up with a way to help her trade her collection of Pez candy dispensers with other Pez collectors. Omidyar says this request was part of the reason he developed the online auction site eBay (formerly known as AuctionWeb), which launched in September 1995. Today, eBay manages auctions for items in 45,000 different categories and has 135 million users. Omidyar is now a billionaire and has started a philanthropical foundation with his Pez-loving ex-girlfriend, now his wife.

From dotcom to dot gone

In the mid-1990s the promise of the World Wide Web as a commercial powerhouse had many entrepreneurs rushing to claim a stake in the new medium. Wall Street and financial analysts were only too happy to fuel the fire, and in a few years investors were pouring billions into the Internet in the hope of striking it rich. But the problem was that many dotcom companies had unrealistic business models. A number of online pet stores, for instance, sold bags of cat litter, which had to be delivered by mail or FedEx – an extremely inefficient way to deliver bulky yet inexpensive items. By the time investors got wise to the folly, companies like Webvan, CGMI, @Home and Metricom had lost billions of dollars. The Web still hasn't recovered from the crash.

LET ME ENTERTAIN YOU

LET ME ENTERTAIN YOU

LET ME ENTERTAIN YOU

LET ME ENTERTAIN YOU

LET ME ENTERTAIN YOU

LET ME ENTERTAIN YOU

LET ME ENTERTAIN YOU

LET ME ENTERTAIN YOU

LET ME ENTERTAIN YOU

LET ME ENTERTAIN YOU

LET ME ENTERTAIN YOU

LET ME ENTERTAIN YOU

LET ME ENTERTAIN YOU

LET ME ENTERTAIN YOU

LET ME ENTERTAIN YOU

LET ME ENTERTAIN YOU

LET ME ENTERTAIN YOU

LET ME ENTERTAIN YOU

LET ME ENTERTAIN YOU

LET ME ENTERTAIN YOU

LET ME ENTERTAIN YOU

LET ME ENTERTAIN YOU

LET ME ENTERTAIN YOU

LET ME ENTERTAIN YOU

LET ME ENTERTAIN YOU

LET ME ENTERTAIN YOU

LET ME ENTERTAIN YOU

LET ME ENTERTAIN YOU

LET ME ENTERTAIN YOU

Computers not only perform useful work for us, they also entertain us. In the days before there were real computers, people created fake computers to star in movies. Today, computers create fake humans to star in movies.

Animation studios such as Pixar and Dreamworks invest millions of dollars developing characters that look almost real. The green-skinned ogre Shrek bends and blinks and walks just like a real ogre does (or would, if ogres were real).

Computer animation gets better every year. You would expect that increasingly realistic and lifelike characters would appeal to movie-goers. Oddly enough, the opposite is proving true. *Polar Express* is a prime example. The hype surrounding the release of *Polar Express* was immense. Magazines and newspapers wrote gushingly about the ultra-realistic computer-generated characters in the film. But when it came out, audiences hated it. They complained that the chararcters were too creepy-looking. What was the problem? Studio executives scratched their heads. The characters in *Polar Express* were more realistic than anything Hollywood had ever created.

And that was precisely the trouble with *Polar Express*. The characters certainly did look more like real people than computed-generated characters from earlier movies, but they didn't look realistic enough to crawl out of the trench of the "Uncanny Valley". That's a term Japanese roboticist Masahiro Mori coined in the late 1970s to describe a graph he developed based on people's reactions to a variety of robot-like objects.

Some of the objects in Mori's tests were non-humanoid, while others were extremely humanoid. Mori discovered that the more lifelike the robot, the more appeal it had – but only up to a point. Past that point, robots that looked sort-of-but-not-quite human were regarded as being extremely weird and unpleasant. They gave off a creepy, jump-started, corpse vibe, and the appeal nosedived.

But even more surprising was the curve beyond the Uncanny Valley. Mori found that when people were shown robots that looked very human, their appeal factor shot way up. People enjoyed these almost-humans most of all.

The Uncannny Valley graph looks like the letter "S" rotated through 90 degrees counterclockwise. It has two peaks. As robots start to look more realistic, so their appeal increases. What kind of robotic creatures are at the first peak? Sony's AIBO robot puppy, for one. It has a cute round puppy shape, but without the facial features, the whiskers or the eyes that are very hard to make natural-looking. If Sony were to add these features, or a pelt, to Aibo's shiny plastic shell, then its appeal would plummet into the Uncanny Valley, because people would regard it as though it were a stuffed dead dog being controlled like a marionette.

But imagine that Sony was able to make a robot dog that looked and behaved exactly like a puppy. Then people would love it. It would be at the top of the second, highest peak, on the other side of the Uncanny Valley.

But computer graphics are nowhere near the other side of the Uncanny Valley yet. Contemporary roboticist Takayasu Sakurai, who is working on developing artificial skin for robots, believes that technological advances will eventually allow robots to climb out of the Uncanny Valley and charm people with their human verisimilitude. He points out that the Mighty Atom (a beloved cartoon character in Japan for 60 years, and known in the USA as Astro Boy) is a perfectly humanlike robot (with some special features, such as jet engines in his feet) and that its popularity among robot researchers makes him "quite optimistic" that the Uncanny Valley will one day be conquered.

Until then, we'll take our entertainment robots on the less realistic side, please.

↦ **Metropolis**

Released in 1926, *Metropolis* shows us a nightmarish world of 2000 in which technology has

run amok. Metropolis is the name of the city where fabulously wealthy people luxuriate without

a thought for the slaves who toil in horrific conditions under the city. When a freedom fighter,

Maria, is captured and locked up by the despotic rulers, she is replaced by a robotic replica

designed to incite a riot among the slaves. Throughout Fritz Lang's masterpiece – which cost

ten times as much to make as other silent films of the time and set a precedent for science

fiction tropes such as bolts of electricity and malformed mad scientists – people and machines

are shown to be inextricably linked to each other, with disastrous consequences.

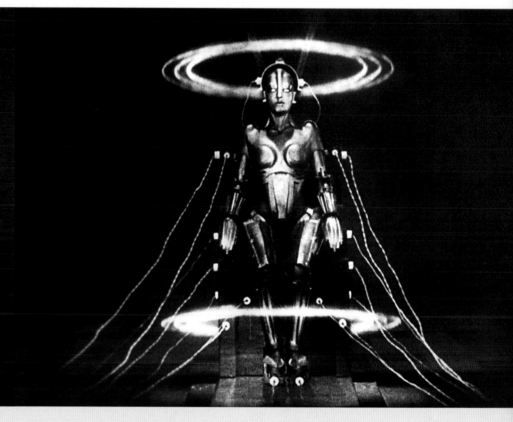

↦ **The Day the Earth Stood Still**

"Gort! Klaatu barada nikto!" If you've ever seen *The Day the Earth Stood Still* (1951), you'll know that this was the famous line used to stop a robot from outer

space from destroying Earth. The story starts when a flying saucer lands in Washington, DC, and a humanoid alien with a North American accent walks down

the ramp that descends dramatically from the UFO. He is accompanied by his 8 ft tall sidekick Gort, who can shoot a death ray from his visor. The humanoid

alien, who is called Klaatu, explains that he has travelled 250 million miles to tell earthlings that if they do not learn to live peacefully, they will be destroyed.

While the irony of using the threat of violence to enforce peace seems to have escaped director Robert Wise (who went on to direct *West Side Story*, *The

Haunting* and *The Sound of Music*) that's exactly the kind of game theory scenario that takes place in the real world. Fun fact: Gort was played by a

7 ft 7 in doorman who worked at Grauman's Chinese Theatre in Hollywood.

824 - 2

Max Mathews

Known as the great-grandfather of techno, Max Mathews (b 1926) wrote a music composition programme called Music I for the IBM 704, when an acoustical researcher at Bell Labs in 1957. The first song lasted just 17 seconds – computers in those days were unable to synthesize music in real time. As computers and software improved, Mathews wrote more complex programmes and songs. He created the first computer singing voice, which sang "A Bicycle Built for Two", the same song later sung by the impaired, demented computer HAL in *2001: A Space Odyssey*. Since 1970, Mathews has focused on developing computerized musical aids for live performance.

Forbidden Planet Robby wasn't the first robot to appear on celluloid, but it's undoubtedly the most memorable. As a co-star in *Forbidden Planet* (1956), Robby had a glass-domed head (so viewers could see its spinning, ticking, electronic brain at work). In the movie, the robot belonged to a scientist who lived with his fetching daughter on an unpopulated planet called Altair-4. Based loosely on William Shakespeare's *The Tempest, Forbidden Planet* tells the story of astronauts sent on a mission to find members of a lost expedition. They're surprised to find the good doctor and his comely daughter living in computer-controlled comfort and attended to by the unfailingly obedient Robby (described in the film as "a housewife's dream"). What the astronauts don't realize is that the planet is lousy, with invisible and deadly monsters.

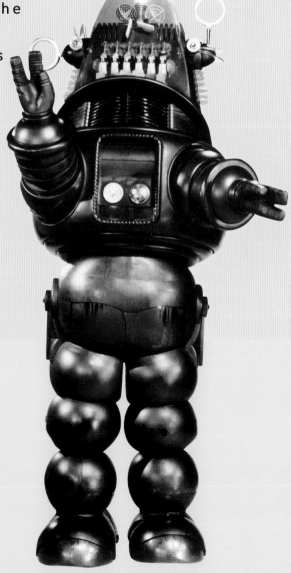

ALPHAVILLE

EDDIE CONSTANTINE

UNE ÉTRANGE AVENTURE DE LEMMY CAUTION

JEAN-LUC GODARD

ANNA KARINA

AKIM TAMIROFF

MUSIQUE DE PAUL MISRAKI

ATHOS FILMS

Desk Set

When the research department of a TV network becomes computerized, good old-fashioned

hilarity ensues in this enjoyable Katharine Hepburn and Spencer Tracy picture called

Desk Set, directed by Walter Lang and based on William Marchant's stage play. The role of

computers in the workplace plays a central role in the movie, as Hepburn's character, the

head of the research department at the Federal Broadcasting Network, resists systems

engineer Tracy's push to automate the network's reference library. The film's computer,

EMMARAC (or "Emmy" as it's affectionately called) is capable of performing tasks that

even today's supercomputers would fail at.

←—| Alphaville

The computer was no hero in the oft-referenced, rarely understood French science fiction movie *Alphaville* (1965), directed by Jean-Luc Godard. The movie pits agent Lemmy Caution against a villainous, sentient computer system called Alpha-60, which is used by Professor von Braun (a thinly veiled reference to rocket scientist Werner von Braun) to brainwash the citizens of Alphaville. Alpha-60 gets hopping mad when Caution hooks up with von Braun's beautiful daughter. Will Caution be able to destroy Alpha-60 before it destroys the lovers' bond? Godard cleverly decided not to use special effects to depict the futuristic Alphaville. Instead, the entire film was shot in exisiting locations around Paris.

Moog synthesizer

After attending an electronic music concert in New York's Greenwich Village in January 1964, an American named Robert Moog set about designing a keyboard-based electronic instrument. He built his first prototype music synthesizer that summer, using a small grant from a local university and with money earned by selling an early type of electronic instrument, called the Theramin, in kit form. While the synthesizer itself didn't contain a computer, its sounds became synonymous with computers and the music it made served as the soundtrack for dozens of science fiction films. Today, vintage Moog synthesizers are highly valued by musicians and collectors.

Wendy Carlos

Composer Wendy Carlos's platinum-selling *Switched on Bach* LP from 1968 introduced the public to electronic music. Although the Moog synthesizer was an analogue device and didn't use computers, it was associated with computers. In 1977 Carlos visited Dartmouth University and saw a digital synthesizer, which inspired her to build her own. Many films featuring computers and robots used Moog synthesizers, and Carlo's music was used in the 1982 Disney movie, *Tron*.

2001: A Space Odyssey

The computer-as-villain was never so brilliantly depicted in cinema as it was by HAL 9000 in Stanley Kubrick's *2001: A Space Odyssey* (1968). Featuring the voice of Douglas Rain, HAL is the computer system that runs a spaceship bound for Jupiter. When the two-man crew realizes that HAL is going insane, they attempt to deactivate it. HAL retaliates by killing one crew member, leaving the survivor to match wits against the self-preserving computer. Kubrick's brilliance shines through in his treatment of HAL as a complex character. When crew member Bowman begins removing critical circuits from the computer, HAL complains: "I'm scared, Dave." Kubrick revisited the issues of humankind's responsibility for its electronic creations three decades later in *AI*. (Incidentally, the letters in "HAL" are one alphabetical step back from "IBM". Kubrick said this was a coincidence, but that's unlikely.)

Colossus: The Forbin Project

In *Colossus: The Forbin Project* (1970), Eric Braeden plays Dr Charles Forbin, the creator of a HAL-like computer designed to control the USA's nuclear weapon system. After locking the super-intelligent computer in an unpenetrable room, Colossus reports that the Russians have built a similar computer, called Guardian. Forbin realizes he's created a monster when the two Cold War computers start up a conversation, decide they're superior to their human makers and begin communicating in an unbreakable secret code. When Russia and the USA sever the connection between the two machines, the computers threaten to annihilate humankind.

Demon Seed

How does a computer get a woman pregnant? When it's an evil super-computer named Proteus IV from the movie *Demon Seed* (1977). When a military scientist decides it's time to pull the plug on a too-smart-for-its-own-good computer, the silicon brain develops an unhealthy obsession with the scientist's estranged wife, played by Julie Christie. After she's mechanically raped by the computer, she becomes pregnant and gives birth to the world's first human-computer hybrid. As dumb as this all sounds (and it is a very dumb film), it touches on a common fear of computers invading what was once the exclusive domain of human beings.

↓ Fairlight CMI

The Fairlight CMI (Computer Musical Instrument) was conceived of in 1975 by a couple of video effects engineers, Kim Ryrie and Peter Vogel, from Australia. They wanted to make a device that could record real music samples and digitally process them to create new sounds. Thus the first digital synthesizer and sampler was born. In 1979 Peter Gabriel and Stevie Wonder were the company's first customers. Gabriel's "Shock The Monkey" was the first hit single to feature the Fairlight CMI, which cost £17,000 without any of the expensive add-ons. Today, digital samplers are commonplace in music studios and cost a fraction of the price of the CMI.

↦ Tron

The Disney movie *Tron* (1982) is the grandad of computer animation films. Starring Jeff Bridges, the film is about a computer programmer who finds himself inside a computer-generated world, foreshadowing the artificial reality of *The Matrix* by a couple of decades. Today, the computer graphics of *Tron* look downright primitive, but at the time, Disney was pushing computer rendering to the limit. The film fared poorly at the box office, though over the years it has become

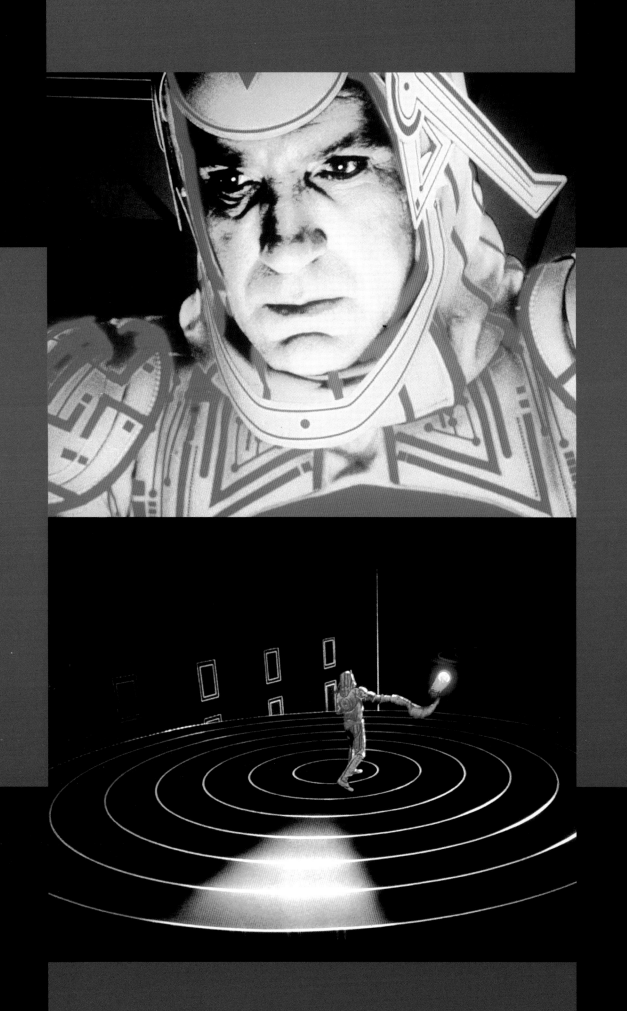

Morphing

In the early 1990s music videos and films became awash with a new computer-driven special effect known as morphing. The word is short for "polymorphic tweening" (tweening is itself derived from "in-between") and it is defined as the seamless transition from one shape to another. Most people's first exposure to morphing was in Michael Jackson's music video *Black or White* (1991), which featured a long sequence of people morphing identities. Morphing is computer-intensive and it was an expensive trick in the 1990s. Today, home video makers can do sophisticated morphing on their personal computers.

The Difference Engine

What would Victorian England have been like if Charles Babbage had succeeded in building his steam-powered computer, called the Difference Engine, and his even more powerful Analytical Engine? That's the question science fiction writers William Gibson and Bruce Sterling ask in their 1989 novel *The Difference Engine*. In this alternate history, the Industrial Revolution and the computer revolution are happening at the same time – and the result is a nineteenth-century smog-choked London filled with mechanical video, ornate robots, steam-driven automobiles and "clackers" (hackers who trade punch-card stacks loaded with viruses).

Pacific Data Images

Computers became a special effects tool in 1980, when Carl Rosendahl, Glenn Entis and Richard Chuang formed Pacific Data Images (PDI) in Sunnyvale, California. Rosendahl developed animation software that ran on minicomputers and his system became a huge hit. In 1985 PDI owned half the computer-generated effects market, creating effects for major TV networks and music videos. Later, PDI created the effects for such movies as *Batman Forever*, *The Arrival*, *Terminator 2* and *Antz*. Carl Rosendahl is shown here developing an animated spot for MTV in 1985.

Toy Story

Pixar's *Toy Story* (1995) was a triumph of computer animation. It served as proof that computers could be used as tools to create engaging, photorealistic worlds and appealing characters. Even today, the film is fresh and enjoyable, thanks in large part to the emphasis on character and story. Unlike earlier films that made extensive use of computer-generated effects, *Toy Story* didn't make a big deal of its techno origins. Instead, the movie invited the viewer to sit back and enjoy a great film that just happened to be made with the help of cutting-edge technology.

The Matrix

Like *Tron*, *The Matrix* (1999) was both made with and about computers. Starring Keanu Reeves as a computer programmer who discovers that the world he lives in is actually an elaborate computer simulation, *The Matrix* featured fantastic computer-generated effects, most notably the "Flow-Mo" process in which actors appeared to hover above the ground as the cameras orbited around them. Flow-Mo was developed by a California-based visual effects facility called Manex. The effect was achieved by first filming the scene with regular film cameras. The images were scanned into a computer, which mapped out a plan for camera placement in the final shot. Then, still cameras were set up along the path. The photographs taken by the still cameras were used much in the same way that animators use key frames to make an animated cartoon. That way, the action could be sped up or slowed down without sacrificing image quality.

AI: Artificial Intelligence

Stanley Kubrick had long wanted to adapt Brian Aldiss's science fiction story *Super-Toys Last All Summer Long* into a film, but he died shortly after getting the project off the ground. It was taken over by Steven Spielberg and released in 2001 as *AI: Artificial Intelligence*. The dark, complex film explores not only the relationship between children and parents, but also between people and the machines on to which they have projected human attributes. Complicating the story even further, Spielberg depicts some of the artificial humans in the film as being capable of having consciousness and others as being clever tricks designed to imitate human nature without having any awareness of what they are doing. Perhaps confusion about this was Spielberg's point.

Polar Express

Sony Imageworks spent an astounding $165 million and employed 500 visual effects specialists to make *Polar Express* (2004), a computer-generated Christmas story. The company used high-profile talent (including Tom Hanks, above) to supply not only the voices of the characters, but also their movements. They used a technique called "motion capture" (mocap, for short). Each actor was covered with 194 shiny plastic "jewels" – 152 of them on the face. Seventy-two special cameras connected to computers recorded the movement of each jewel. The captured data was used to generate the movement of the animated characters.

Napster and the birth of music trading systems When 18-year-old college student Shawn Fanning unleashed the

music-sharing programme Napster in 1999, it blindsided the recorded music industry. By 2000 Napster had

38 million users worldwide, and the network was growing at a rate of one million new users a day, none of

whom paid a single cent for the music they were downloading. The music industry went to court and

successfully shut Napster's central server down, effectively killing it. But a dozen new music-trading systems

popped up in its place and none of them used a central database, which made them almost impossible to

shut down. Today, the music industry tries to control the problem by identifying and prosecuting individuals

who trade music, but it is fighting a losing battle.

iPod   Apple introduced the first iPod on 10 November 2001, at a price of US$399. With a 5GB hard drive (enough to store about 1,000 songs) and a brilliantly elegant scroll-wheel control interface, the music player was a critical success, but the high price kept many away. Only 125,000 were sold by the end of the year. But as prices dropped and capacity went up, iPod fever hit. George W. Bush uses one, as do many people working at Apple arch-rival Microsoft. Today, more than seven million iPods have been sold and Apple is now more famous as a music-player company than as a computer company.

THE WORLD OF TOMORROW
THE WORLD OF TOMORROW
THE WORLD OF TOMORROW
THE WORLD OF TOMORROW
THE WORLD OF TOMORROW
THE WORLD OF TOMORROW
THE WORLD OF TOMORROW
THE WORLD OF TOMORROW
THE WORLD OF TOMORROW
THE WORLD OF TOMORROW
THE WORLD OF TOMORROW
THE WORLD OF TOMORROW
THE WORLD OF TOMORROW
THE WORLD OF TOMORROW
THE WORLD OF TOMORROW
THE WORLD OF TOMORROW
THE WORLD OF TOMORROW
THE WORLD OF TOMORROW
THE WORLD OF TOMORROW
THE WORLD OF TOMORROW
THE WORLD OF TOMORROW
THE WORLD OF TOMORROW
THE WORLD OF TOMORROW
THE WORLD OF TOMORROW
THE WORLD OF TOMORROW
THE WORLD OF TOMORROW
THE WORLD OF TOMORROW
THE WORLD OF TOMORROW
THE WORLD OF TOMORROW
THE WORLD OF TOMORROW
THE WORLD OF TOMORROW

U.S. AIR FORCE

The future of computers is ripe with possibilities. Quantum computing, holographic storage, personal area networks, flexible displays, location-sensing technologies... The list is endless. But the field that's most appealing is robots – humanoid robots, to be specific. The human race just can't seem to shake off its fascination with making life from a machine.

Despite decades of effort, humanoid robots have yet to make the leap from laboratories to our homes. But thanks to ever-cheaper computing power and intensive efforts by Japanese companies, humanoid robots are on the way. Sony's QRIO, Honda's Asimo, Toyota's Partner Robot and Mitsubishi's Wakamaru are the four bipeds of the robocalypse, tottering across convention hall stages around the world. They may not be at your doorstep yet, but they're coming.

The humanoids' predecessors, industrial robots, have been around since the early 1960s, assembling everything from wristwatches to bulldozers. Today, they're a US$5.6 billion industry, with 720,000 "working robots" toiling in factories around the world. Relatively speaking, industrial robots are easy to build. They're programmed for specific tasks, such as painting cars. Weight and power considerations aren't a problem. They don't have to move anywhere.

Contrast that with the challenges a home robot has to deal with. It needs to be able to sense and respond to the ever-changing world around it, avoiding obstacles, preventing injury to itself and people, keeping its balance when walking on different kinds of terrain and carrying its own power supply, actuator system and computer. These aren't simple problems to solve. Researchers don't fully understand how humans do all these things, never mind trying to recreate those behaviours in a robot.

But to the extent that anyone is figuring this out, it's Sony, with five years of experience selling the world's most complex mass-produced domestibot, the US$2,000 AIBO. The latest incarnation of Sony's plastic puppy, the AIBO ERS-7, can freely roam about your house, finding and fetching a toy bone, accepting Web-initiated commands to take pictures and recognizing individual human faces. When its battery pack runs low, it can find its power charging station and plug itself in. More than 130,000 AIBOs have been sold worldwide since the robotic pooch arrived in 1999.

AIBO is just Sony's first step into the home robot market. Its current project, a 61 cm (2 ft) tall biped named QRIO (pronounced "curio") represents the culmination of seven years of work by some of Japan's leading roboticists. The world's number one consumer electronics firm hopes that the robotics technology it develops will lead not only to better domestic robots, but also to mind-bogglingly wonderful devices endowed with robot-like capabilities, such as DVD recorders you can talk to, or computers that sense changes in the outside world and adjust your schedule accordingly. And once QRIO's fingers get stronger, it'll pick up a PSX controller and kick your butt in Grand Theft Auto. If Sony has its way, everything produced by the US$70 billion company will have a little bit of QRIO in it.

But it's extraordinarily difficult to make an autonomous, two-legged robot. It's a hundred times more complicated than the animatronic president-bots at

Disneyland. The robotic Abe Lincoln may rise out of its chair, but it's nothing more than a refinement over the cuckoo clock or the pianola. Mechano-Abe doesn't need to see objects in three dimensions in order to get them or avoid them. It doesn't need to make an internal map of its immediate environment. It doesn't need to be continually adjusting its skeletomuscular anatomy to keep from falling.

But QRIO has to do all this and more. When I visited Sony robot headquarters in June 2004, I watched an engineer push his palm against QRIO's chest in an attempt to knock it over. QRIO's response was startlingly lifelike – it adjusted its posture and managed to keep from tipping over. Then the engineer gave QRIO a hard shove, and the robot tucked in its limbs and sort of rolled down as a way to protect itself. After lying inertly for a few seconds, it clambered back up on its feet, ready for more abuse.

In the real world, an impressive engineering hack doesn't necessarily equate to a market opportunity. Home robots could very well be a solution in search of a problem. Who really needs a home robot? Or, more specifically, how wonderful will home robots have to be before everybody wants one?

Some Japanese companies are approaching the problem by developing home robots for a specific market: the elderly. Because of Japan's low birth rate (most families have just one child), the population is getting greyer by the year. Japan's National Livelihood Survey, issued in August 2003, revealed that out of Japan's 21 million people over the age of 65, more than three million live alone. The country is looking seriously at robots as a way to take care of and provide companionship for the elderly, doing everything from dispensing medicine to changing nappies.

Toyota and several other companies say their efforts in this field are geared towards developing robots that will one day assist in hospitals and care homes for the elderly by delivering meals, controlling TV sets and monitoring the halls.

Toshiyo Tamura, a professor of gerontechnology at the National Institute for Longevity Sciences in Obu, in Japan, conducts robot-therapy sessions with Alzheimer's patients in hospitals, using AIBO robots dressed in soft clothing. Tamura says the AIBOs have a profoundly positive effect on patients, especially those in the late stages of Alzheimer's. "We focus on the elderly who are severe dementia patients," he says. "The problems of such patients are wandering and agitation during daily life. We are trying to improve their quality of life. Although severe dementia patients do not know themselves – that is, they forget their name – they have human feelings. Thus we try to heal them so they can spend the rest of life happy."

When I was at Sony's robot labs, I asked Satoshi Amagai, the division president, what was Sony's ultimate goal with robots. His answer was surprising: "We would like to create a personal robot that has a strong affinity for humans".

In other words, Sony doesn't want to make a robot that we can love; it wants to make a robot that can love us.

↧ Haptic interfaces

Computers do a good job of sending sound and images to our eyes and ears, but they fail miserably at delivering the sensations of touch to our skin. That's where haptics comes in. From the Greek word meaning "to touch", haptic computer interfaces can transmit the sensations of, among other things, textures, vibrations, stickiness and explosions. Haptic interfaces are already available in medical training equipment and on some game platforms. The haptic arm-wrestling machine shown here allows people who are separated geographically to arm wrestle each other via an Internet connection. Other potential applications for haptics include devices that would let you feel the texture of a fabric displayed on a website by running your finger across a haptic touchpad.

Smart dust ↑

Imagine computers so tiny that they look like particles of dust. Researchers at the University of California at Berkeley call them smart dust. These subminiature computers (today, they're the size of aspirin tablets, but they'll get smaller in the years to come) are equipped with sensors that can measure environmental conditions. Motes of smart dust can be installed in shipping warehouses, bird sanctuaries, lakes – any location that needs to be monitored for changes in temperature, humidity, pollution or any other measurable phenomenon. Each sensor contains a radio transmitter and receiver, and can communicate with other nearby sensors. The data hops from sensor to sensor, eventually making its way to a central computer, where it can be analyzed.

-14.9

81T172M1_

It was the painter's last commission.

Position 123.0 -12.5
Target
Current Point_181T172M1_
Distance 1

Augmented Reality

Augmented Reality is a way to add an extra layer of information on top of the real world. By wearing special transparent goggles that can project visual data directly on to your retina, you may one day be able to walk through an unfamiliar city, following the glowing arrows and paying heed to the information that's displayed on top of streets, restaurants and landmarks, which only you can see. Today, some pilots have "heads-up" displays installed in the windscreens of their planes to allow them to see maps and runway configurations superimposed over the terrain below, even if it is dark or cloudy outside.

Wireframe
Hidden Line
Filled

Point 157_   Point 160_
Point 151_
Point 139_
126T139M1_

tion:
361

Target   Point 189

Point 180
Point 186
Point 157

Location:
96.9901

Target   Gusshausstrasse 27

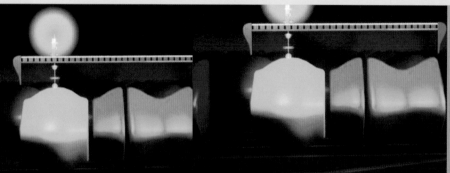

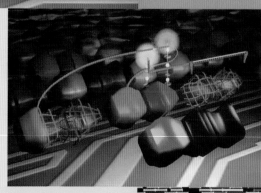

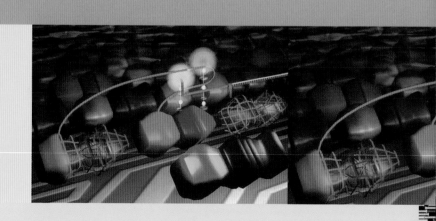

Artificial life

Artificial Intelligence research, or AI, has been around for 50 years now, but it has proved to

be a tough nut to crack. Why have researchers been unable to synthesize intelligent decision

making in a computer? One reason is that life is too unpredictable and open-ended for a

computer programme to be able to respond appropriately to anything thrown at it. About 15

years ago, some computer scientists and biologists decided to take a different approach to

creating intelligence – by imitating nature. This technology is called "artificial life", or a-life.

By allowing programmes to evolve in ways similar to how plants and animal species adapt,

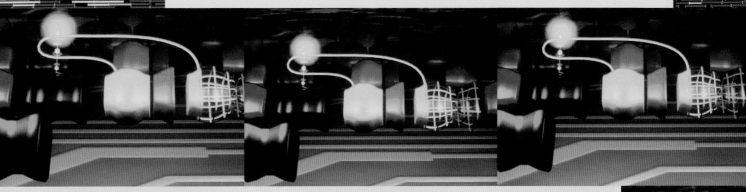

surprising complex behaviours in programmes can be developed. Today, a-life techniques are used to make

realistic-looking lifeforms in films and television. In the future, a-life software might power the brains of

domestic robots.

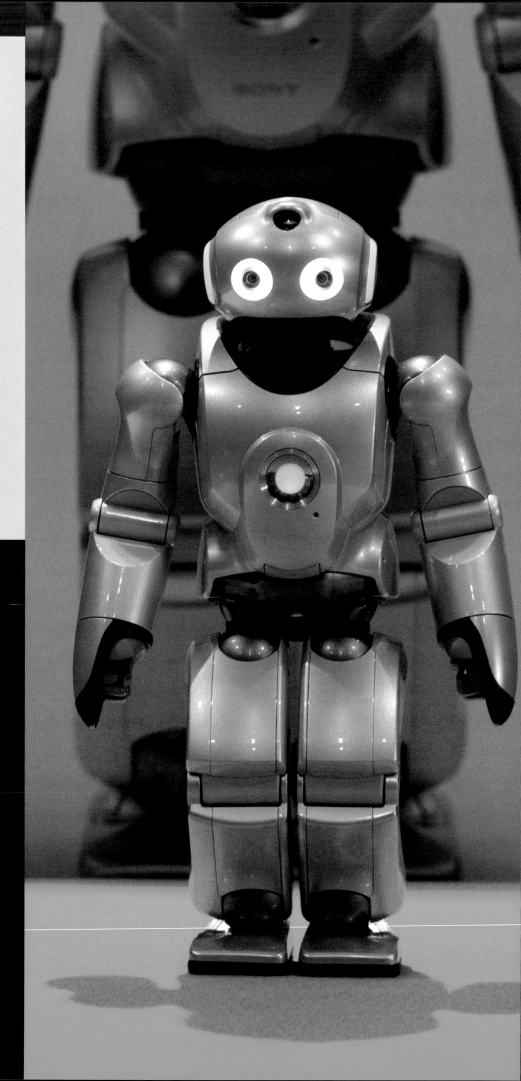

⊢→ QRIO

QRIO, introduced in 2004, is Sony's robotic goodwill ambassador – "a 'partner' that talks to you, plays with you, encourages you". Resembling a toddler in a shiny spacesuit, QRIO has 38 motors and several onboard computers to endow it with astonishingly lifelike behaviour. It can walk across uneven surfaces, dance, run (albeit slowly) and chase after a ball. If it falls down, it uses its limbs to protect itself from damage, then gets back up on its own. It uses a 3D vision system to navigate around obstacles and can recognize people's faces. Sony says it has no plans to put QRIO on the market – at least, not at this time.

⊢→ ⊢→ AIBO

It won't chew the furniture or wake you in the middle of the night to be let outside, but it will play fetch, perform tricks and communicate with your computer. Sony's AIBO ERS-7 is a robotic puppy dog with an onboard wireless microprocessor. It has sensors built into its nose and chest to help it avoid walls and obstacles. When its battery runs low, this US$2,000 quadruped can find its recharging station and juice itself up. Out of the box, the robot knows very little, but it soon learns to recognize its owner's face and voice, and will respond to a variety of commands. Much to Sony's consternation, AIBO owners have learned to modify the robot's personality by tweaking its software and they trade modification tips on the Internet.

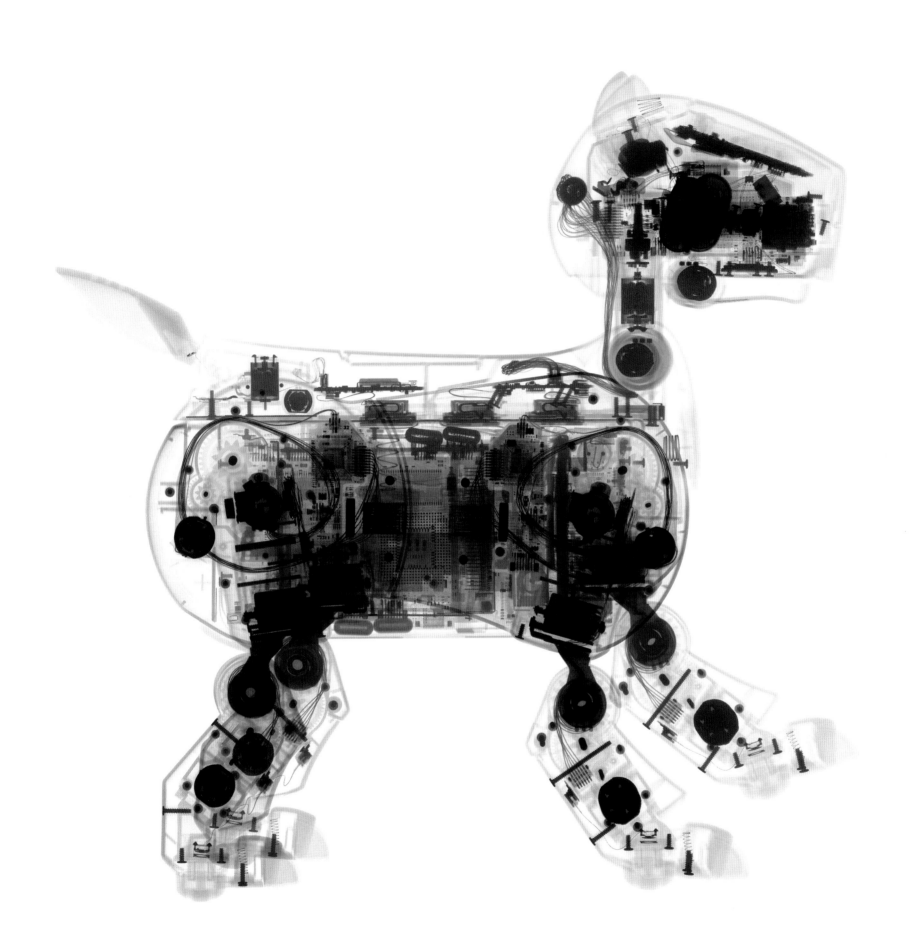

Implants for the human brain

In the future, when your brain starts to fail, you might be able to replace the broken parts with a computer implant. Theodore Berger, a researcher at the University of Southern California, has developed a microchip that emulates a portion of the brain called the hippocampus, which helps the brain memorize. In 2004 Berger successfully demonstrated the chip when he wired it up to living brain tissue taken from a rat. Berger and other implant researchers hope that implants will one day be used to treat people with Alzheimer's disease, Parkinson's disease and other neurological disorders.

Ambient devices

Do you want to check up on how your stock investment is doing, or learn what the weather is like in Paris? With an ambient device, you don't need to go to your computer to find out – you can just glance at the special frosted-glass bulb on your desk. If it's blue, that means your portfolio is safe, or that the skies over Paris are clear. But if the light is red, then you better call your broker, or consider cancelling your planned weekend trip to the Continent. Researchers at the Massachusetts Institute of Technology's Media Lab have formed a company, called Ambient Devices, to sell everyday devices that deliver information in novel ways. The devices receive wireless data and convert it into analogue signals that can be displayed as changing colours in a light or the movement of a needle in a meter.

⊢→ Quantum computers

The computer on your desk uses computer architecture principles that go back 60 years. Your computer and Konrad Zuse's computers of the 1940s differ only in size and speed – yours is a lot smaller and a lot more powerful. But computers are reaching the limits of miniaturization and speed using current technology. That's why researchers have been so interested in quantum computing. An ordinary computer works with bits – ones and zeros – but a quantum computer would use a qubit, which has additional states. By exploiting the behaviour of physics at the submicroscopic level, quantum computers have the potential to be much faster than conventional computers. It would be possible, for instance, to use a quantum computer to unscramble almost instantly encoded messages that would take thousands of years to unscramble using today's fastest supercomputers. To date, a number of limited experiments with quantum computing have been successful.

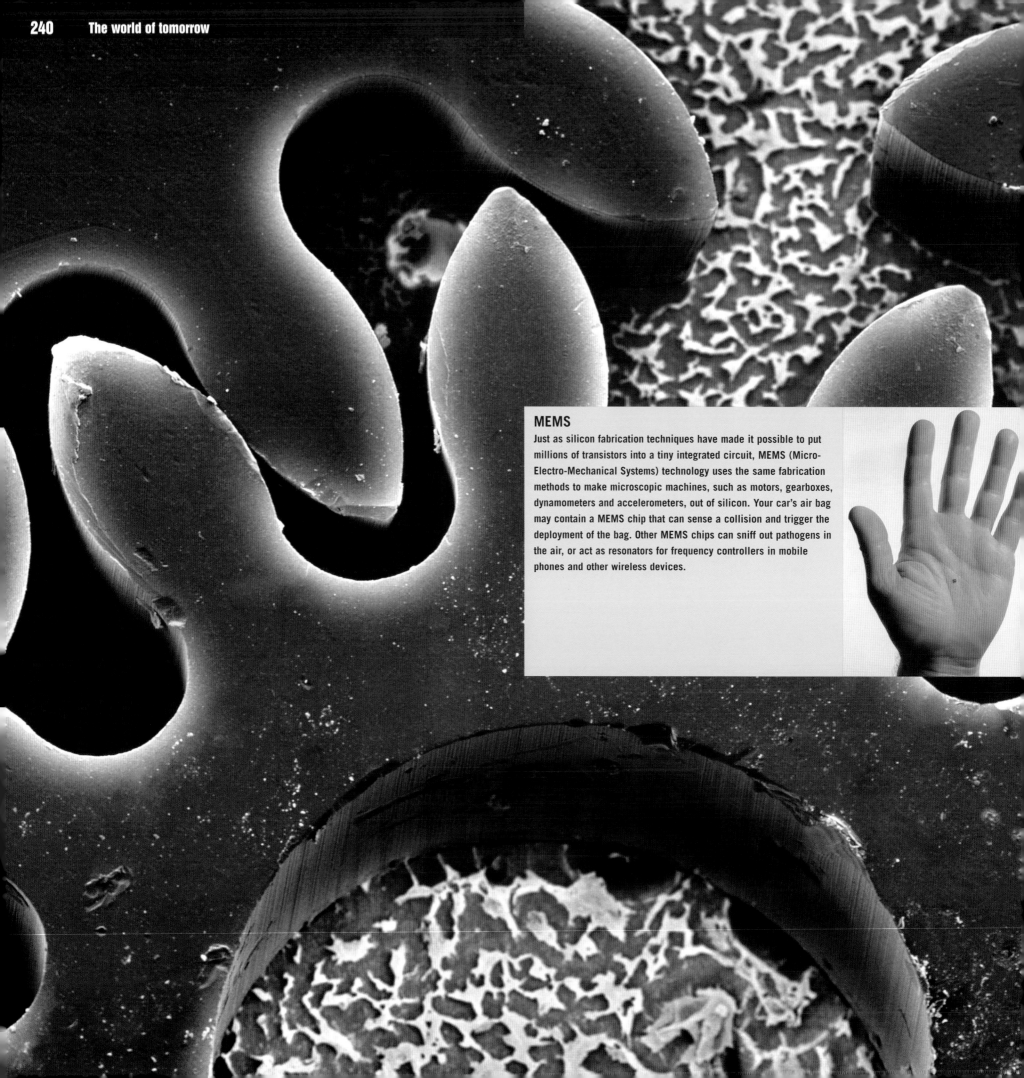

MEMS

Just as silicon fabrication techniques have made it possible to put millions of transistors into a tiny integrated circuit, MEMS (Micro-Electro-Mechanical Systems) technology uses the same fabrication methods to make microscopic machines, such as motors, gearboxes, dynamometers and accelerometers, out of silicon. Your car's air bag may contain a MEMS chip that can sense a collision and trigger the deployment of the bag. Other MEMS chips can sniff out pathogens in the air, or act as resonators for frequency controllers in mobile phones and other wireless devices.

Unmanned ground vehicles

Why send a human into a dangerous situation, such as a building that might contain terrorists, when you can send in a robot instead? That's the idea behind unmanned ground vehicles (UGVs), which are being developed at military research labs around the world. UGVs come in two varieties – ones that can move about under their own control, and others that serve as eyes and ears for an operator stationed in a safe area. Both types can wirelessly transmit video, audio and other types of data, but autonomous UGVs are also equipped with collision avoidance and threat assessment sub-systems so they can make decisions without human intervention. The six-wheeled Mars Exploration Rover, shown here, has a semi-autonomous navigation system that allows it to plan local routes after receiving earthbound instructions to drive to a specifc location.

↑ Holographic data storage

Storage media such as tapes and disks retain their data on the surface of the material. But holographic storage penetrates the surface and uses the entire thickness of the disc to store information, thus offering extremely high storage density. Holographic storage could also prove to be much faster than disks because multiple bits can be written simultaneously with a single pulse of laser light. The problem holding back laser storage is the lack of a suitable medium on which to read and write data, but in April 2005 InPhase Technologies in Las Vegas, Nevada, announced that it had demonstrated data densities of 200 gigabits per square inch on a special kind of plastic disk using holographic storage. The company claims it will have a 1.6 terabyte (a terabyte is 1,000 gigabytes) holographic disk for sale by 2009.

←┤ Unmanned aerial vehicles

Planes without pilots? It sounds frightening, but unmanned aerial vehicles (UAVs) are already here. First developed for the military (as seen here), UAVs are soaring into the private sector. One of the most novel is a solar-powered aeroplane called SkyTower that flies above the stratosphere and acts like a very-low-altitude satellite for telecommunications. SkyTower can be piloted by a person on the ground, while an on-board Macintosh computer manages immediate control requirements. In 2002 SkyTower successfully flew over Hawaii and transmitted data to laptop computers and mobile phones on the ground.

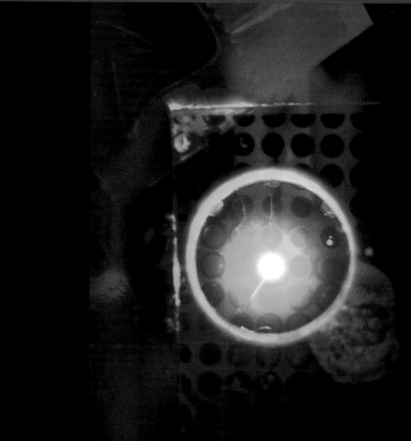

Electronic digital paper

Typical computer displays use television-style tubes or liquid crystal displays (LCDs), but a growing number of companies are working on alternatives. Electronic digital paper, also known as bistable displays, or e-paper, uses electrostatically charged coloured balls floating in a white liquid, which is sandwiched between layers of glass or plastic. The result is a high-resolution display that looks as good as real paper. Another big advantage of e-paper is that the display needs no power to show an image – power is required only when the image is changed. Even when the power is shut off, the image remains. This will greatly increase the battery life of mobile devices that use e-paper displays.

Organic Light Emitting Diodes

The main problem with today's LCD displays (the flat-panel displays found in laptops) is that they require a backlight so you can see the image. Backlights consume a lot of power, which means a shorter battery life for portable computers. But a new kind of display, called an OLED (Organic Light Emitting Diodes) display, will change that. As the name suggests, OLEDs generate their own light and require significantly less power than a backlight. OLEDs are also brighter and sharper than LCDs, and have faster refresh rates, which reduces eyestrain. The main challenge with OLEDs is preventing the pigments from fading over time. So far, a few mobile phone manufacturers have offered phones with OLED displays. In the coming years, laptop computer makers will start to offer OLEDs in their products.

Personal Area Network

Wide Area Networks (WANs) connect computers across long distances. Local Area Networks (LANs) connect computers at a single facility. Personal Area Networks (PANs) connect the devices you carry with you. When you take a picture with your digital camera, it will connect to the global positioning satellite system in your pocket and add the latitude and longitude to the photograph's description. When you pull your handheld computer out of your other pocket, it will download the photograph from your camera so you can email it to a friend. When your mobile phone rings, it will send a signal to mute your music player. And when two people meet, they can link their pans and share data if they agree on it.

Your life in photographs

How would you like to have a complete record of your entire life's experiences stored as a series of photographs? Whether you want to or not, researchers at Microsoft are developing a system called MyLifeBits that will automatically record everything you do and store it on a computer for easy retrieval. The heart of the system is a small digital camera, called the SenseCam, which has a number of sensors that try to detect when a good photograph opportunity presents itself and cause the camera to snap a picture. The researchers hope that such a system would make casual photography an unconscious act, so you wouldn't have to take yourself "out of the moment" to snap a photograph of your child performing in a school play, for instance. And if you have so much fun at the Christmas party that you can't remember what happened, you can use the system to review your behaviour in the sober light of the following morning.

Roll-out handheld displays

A common complaint about handheld computers is that the displays are too small. Today, mobile phone operators are offering television and films, but they must be viewed on the phone's 5 cm (2 in) screen, which makes the experience less than cinematic. In the future, this problem could be solved by adding a flexible display that will roll out of a slot in the side of the device, much like a window blind, to provide a 12.7 cm (5 in) display. PolymerVision in the Netherlands has developed a display that uses plastic instead of the customary glass as the base for the materials needed to make a high-resolution display. This makes the screen so flexible that it can be rolled up and stowed away out of sight until needed.

RFID chips

RFID chips are tiny radios that transmit a unique identification number when electrically charged. Today, RFID chips are implanted under the skin of livestock and pets. Several countries around the world are implanting the chips in people, as a form of identification. In Mexico RFIDs are being implanted in children as a way to discourage kidnappings. As the price of RFID chips falls, they'll be added to products and grocery items to facilitate inventory control. Your refrigerator could also monitor what you put in it and generate a grocery list when provisions run low.

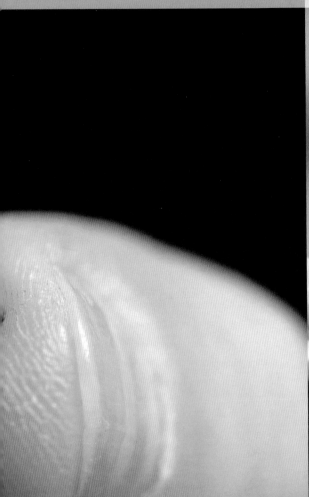
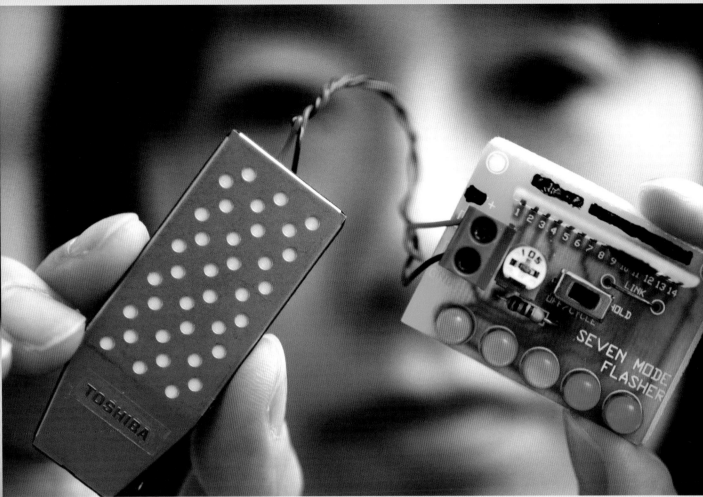

Fuel cells

As technology becomes increasingly mobile, battery life will become an important issue. Unlike other components in computers – processors and memory – battery life technology doesn't become twice as powerful every year and a half. Battery technology advances much more slowly. But fuel cells offer an alternative to batteries. They look like batteries, but they create electrical energy by taking oxygen out of the air and combining it with hydrogen in fuel. Instead of recharging them as you would a battery, you simply pour more fuel (even vodka could be used) into the fuel cell and you're good to go. In late 2004 Toshiba made the world's smallest fuel cell, suitable for use in handheld gadgets.

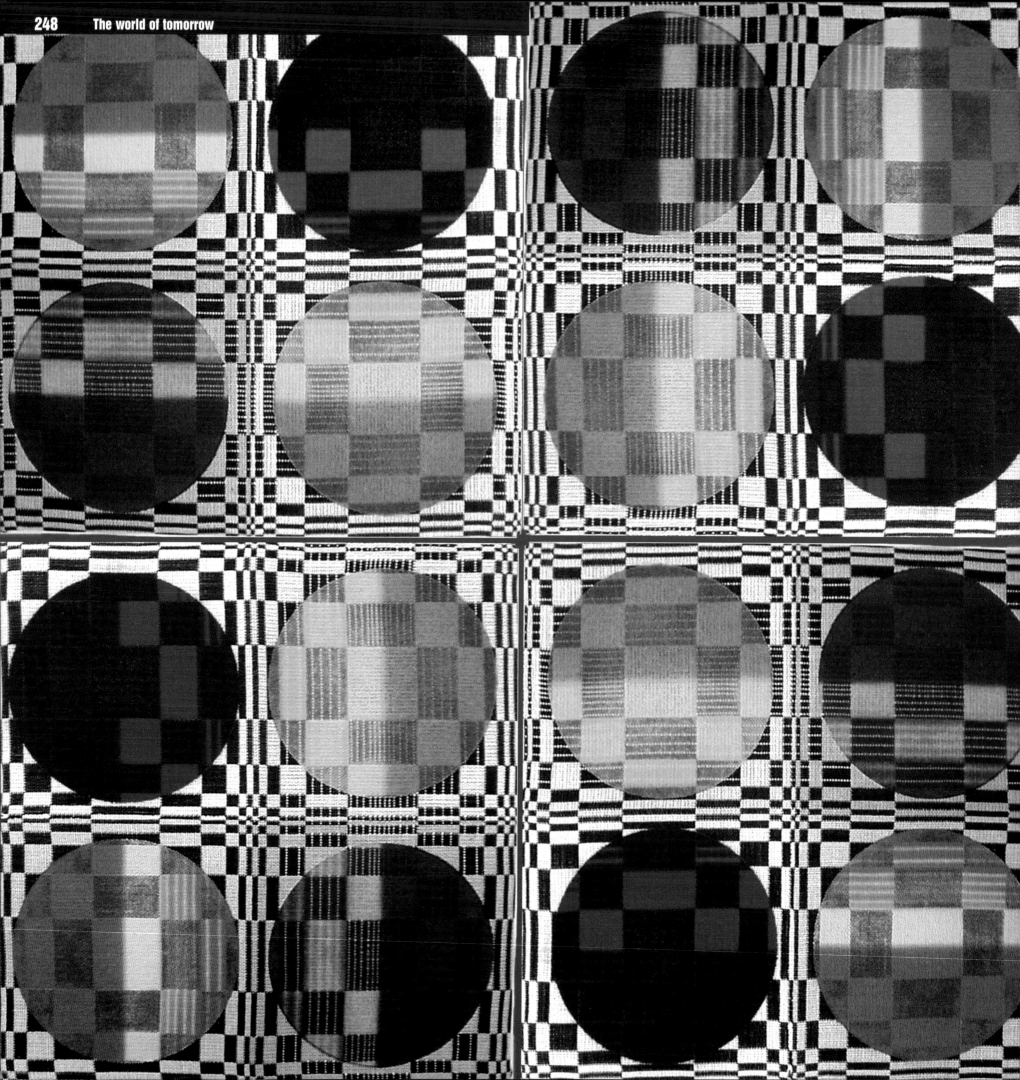

Electronic textiles could allow you to change your clothes without changing your clothes.

International Fashion Machines, a company in Seattle, Washington, makes electronic fabrics that can display animated digital images (shown here). These hand-woven computer displays – sold as wall hangings – can change colours and patterns with the push of a button. Parisian fashion designer Elisabeth De Senneville created a line of garments that display video game characters using flexible colour screens developed by France Telecom.

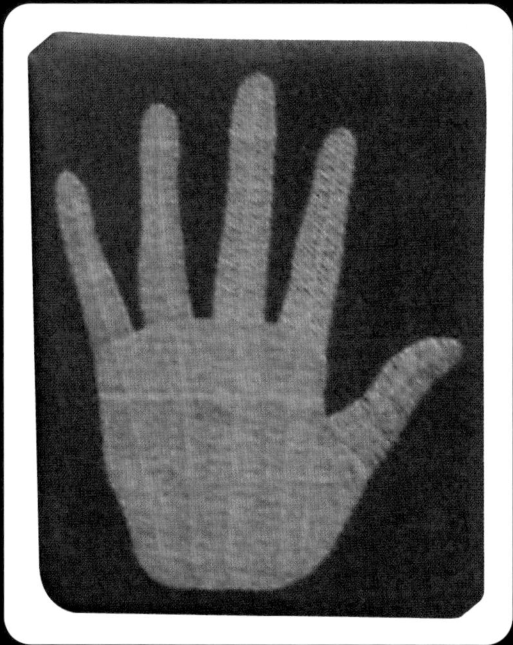

⟵ Worker robots

Industrial robots have been part of the international workforce for decades, but worker robots – the kind that can walk or wheel themselves around houses, streets and factories – have, until very recently, been the sole province of science fiction. Improvements in robot locomotion, sensors and computer technology have unleashed a crop of semi-autonomous humanoid robots that guard warehouses and shoot intruders with plastic balls, assist people at the post office, and tend to patients in hospitals and nursing homes. Japan, with its ageing population, is especially keen on finding ways to take care of its elderly citizens and is looking seriously at robots as a solution.

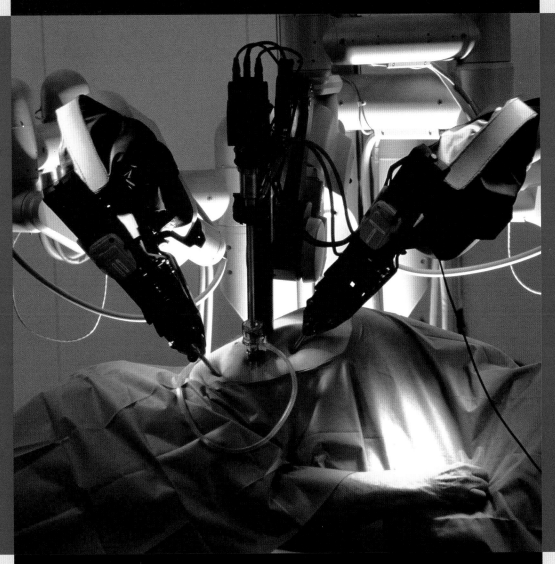

↑ Telesurgery

Telemedicine – remotely diagnosing and treating people who are ill – has been around at least since the advent of television. But until recently, telemedicine and robot-assisted medicine hasn't been practical. With the arrival of high-speed Internet, however, it's becoming a reality. A robot-surgeon called Da Vinci (shown here) is used to perform minimally invasive heart surgery. The doctor remotely controls the robot, using a real-time three-dimensional image of the heart to guide him or her. And in 2005 Israel's Tactile Technologies developed a robotic "self-guiding" dental drill that is controlled by the dentist using a personal computer with a wireless radio. While both of these examples require the doctor to be present in the same room as the patient, it's only a matter of time before surgical procedures will take place without the surgeon or patient ever meeting.

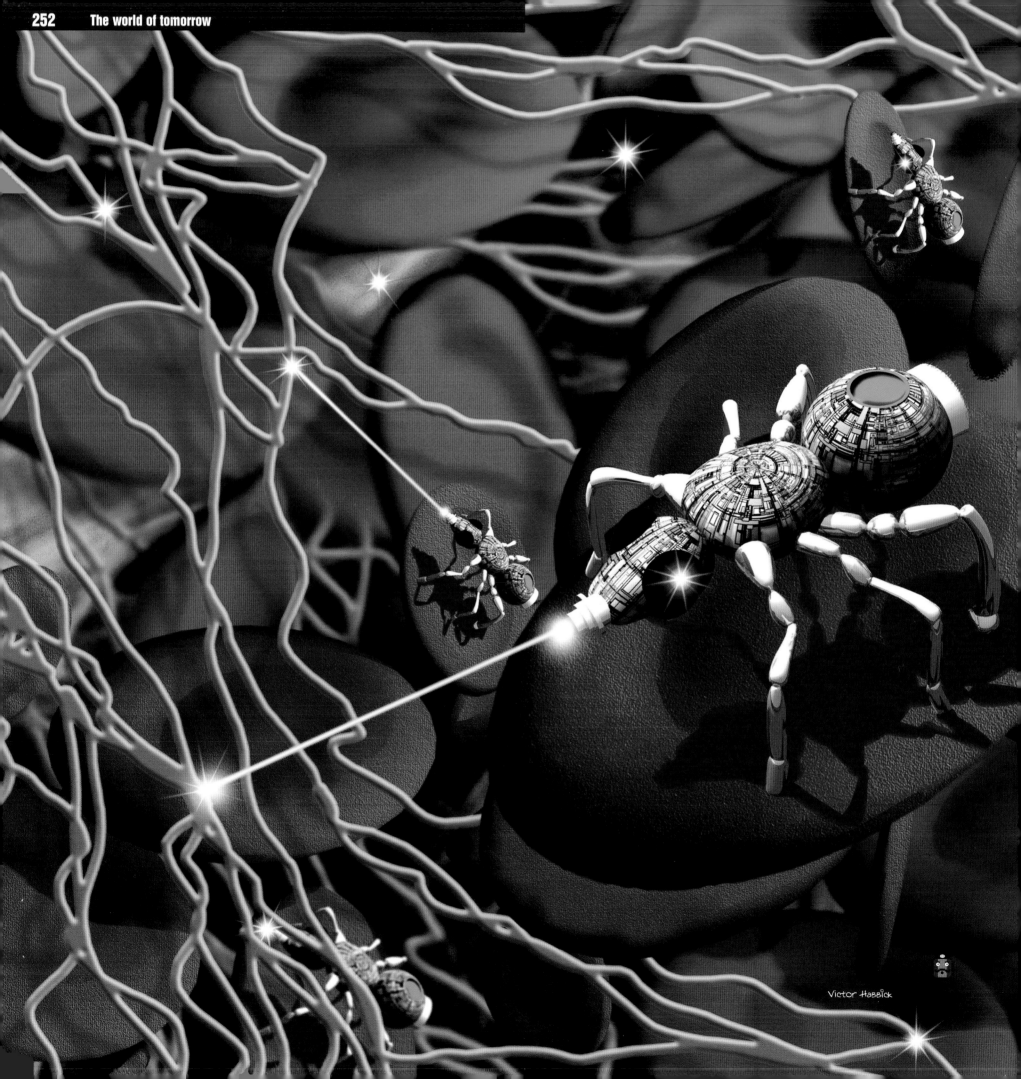

Victor Habbick

Nanomedicine

Nanotechnology is the science of making machines on the molecular level. It has already shown promise in certain applications, such as construction materials, textiles and electronics, but one of the long-term goals is nanomedicine – using tiny machines to monitor and repair humans at the sub-cellular level. Researchers envision injecting patients with a dose of microscopic robots that would propel themselves through the bloodstream, looking for cancerous cells to destroy or damaged DNA to repair. The image shown here is a concept illustration of a nanomedicine robot using a laser beam to break up an abnormal blood clot.

Index

Credits

The publishers would like to thank the following sources for their kind permission to reproduce the pictures in the book:

2: Brookhaven National Laboratory (top), IBM Corporate Archives (centre & bottom); 3: Science Photo Library/Gusto; 6: Science & Society Picture Library/Science Museum; 7: Science Photo Library Picture Library/Victor Habbick Visions; 12-13: Corbis/ Horace Bristol; 16: Corbis/Gianni Dagli Orti; 17: Corbis/Nik Wheeler; 18: Science & Society Picture Library/Science Museum; 19: Corbis/Horace Bristol; 20: The Bridgeman Art Library/Bibliotheque Nationale, Paris, France; 20-21: Science & Society Picture Library/Science Museum; 21: Corbis/Gianni Dagli Orti; 22–3: Science & Society Picture Library/Science Museum; 24: Science Photo Library/George Bernard; 24–5: Corbis/Bettmann; 26: Science & Society Picture Library/Science Museum Pictorial (left), Science Photo Library (right); 27: www.jeff560tripod.com; 28: Corbis/Archivo Icongrafico, S.A. ; 29: Science Photo Library; 30–31: Topfoto.co.uk; 31: Science Photo Library; 32: Science Photo Library; 33: Science & Society Picture Library/Science Museum; 34: Private Collection (bottom right), Science Photo Library (top right); 35: Science & Society Picture Library/Science Museum; 36: Science & Society Picture Library/Science Museum (left), Science Photo Library/Shelia Terry (top right); 37: Courtesy of Ehuelamo@telfonica.net (top left), Science & Society Picture Library/Science Museum (top right); 38-39: Science Photo Library; 42: Science & Society Picture Library/Science Museum; 43: Science Photo Library (top left), Topfoto.co.uk/Ann Ronan Picture Library/HIP (bottom right); 44: Science Photo Library/Dr. Jeremy Burgess; 44-45: Science Photo Library; 46: Rex Features/Richard Gardner; 47-49: Science Photo Library; 49: Corbis/Bettmann (right); 50-51: Rex Features/Roger-Viollet; 52-53: Science Photo Library; 54: Corbis/Hulton-Deutsch Collection; 58: Corbis/Bettmann; 59: Science Photo Library/Shelia Terry; 60: Topfoto.co.uk; 61: Topfoto.co.uk (left), IBM Corporate Archives (right); 62: Corbis/Hulton-Deutsch Collection; 63: MIT Museum (top), IBM Corporate Archives (bottom); 64: Science Photo Library; 65: AKG-Images/Ullstein Bild (left), Science Photo Library/© Estate of Francis Bello (right); 66: Zuse Multimedia Andwendungen; 66-67: MIT Museum; 68-69: Corbis/Bettmann; 72: Topfoto.co.uk (left), Corbis/Bettmann (top right); 73: Topfoto.co.uk/PA; 74–5: Science Photo Library/Los Alamos National Laboratory; 76: Topfoto.co.uk; 77: Zuse Multimedia Andwendungen; 78: Corbis/Bettmann (left), Science Photo Library (right) & Photos12.com/Naval Surface Weapons Centre; 79: Corbis/Bettmann; 80: Topfoto.co.uk; 81: Science & Society Picture Library (top left), Corbis/Bettmann (top right); 82–3: IBM Corporate Archives; 87: Topfoto.co.uk; 88: Science Photo Library/Alfred Pasieka; 89: Topfoto.co.uk; 90: Corbis/Bettmann; 91: Topfoto.co.uk; 92: Corbis/Bettmann; 93: Science & Society Picture Library/Science Museum, Topfoto.co.uk (right); 94: Science & Society Picture Library/Science Museum/Mitre Corporation; 94–5: Corbis/Bettmann; 96: Getty Images/Time Life Pictures (left), Zuse Multimedia Andwendungen (right); 97: Topfoto.co.uk; 98–9: Science Photo Library/Volker Steger; 100–02: IBM Corporate Archives; 103: Picture-Desk/Image courtesy of The Advertising Archives; 104–05: Corbis/Bettmann; 106: Picture-Desk/Image courtesy of The Advertising Archives; 107: Science Photo Library/Novosti; 108: Science & Society Picture Library/NMPFT Daily Herald Archive; 109: Getty Images/Henry Grosinsky/Time Life Pictures; 110–11: Science Photo Library/Volker Steger; 111: Private Collection; 112–13: Corbis/Deborah Feingold; 116–17: VintageTech; 118–19: www.computercollector.com; 120: VintageTech; 121: Bootstrap Institute; 122: Computer History Museum (left), Science Photo Library/Volker Steger (right); 123: Science Photo Library/Volker Steger; 124: Corbis/Roger Ressmeyer (left), Corbis/Ed Kashi (right); 125: Corbis/Roger Ressmeyer; 126: VintageTech (left), IBM Corporate Archive (right); 127: Erik Klein/www.vintage-computer.com (left), Courtesy of Palo Alto Research Center (right); 128: Corbis/Doug Wilson (left), Hewlett Packard Museum (right); 129: Getty Images/Xerox; 130: Courtesy of Palo Alto Research Center (top left), www.bkblackburn.com (bottom right); 131: www.vintage-computer.com (top left), Private Collection (bottom right); 132: Getty Images/Diana Walker/Liaison; 132–3: Science Photo Library/Peter Menzel; 134: Topfoto.co.uk; 134–5: IBM Corporate Archives; 135: Science Photo Library/Volker Steger; 136: Topfoto.co.uk (left), Corbis/Roger Ressmeyer (right); 136–7: Topfoto.co.uk; 138: Corbis/Roger Ressmeyer; 139: Topfoto.co.uk; 140: Enrico Tedeschi (left), Science Photo Library (right); 141: Corbis; 142: Picture-Desk/Images courtesy of Advertising Archives; 143: IBM Corporate Archives; 144: VintageTech; 145: Science Photo Library/Andrew McClenaghan; 146: Picture-Desk/Images courtesy of Advertising Archives; 147: Corbis/Ed Kashi; 148: Getty Images/Time Life Pictures; 149: Science & Society Picture Library/Science Museum; 150: Getty Images/Time Life Pictures/John Harding; 151: Getty Images/Shahn Kermani/Liaison; 152: Corbis/Deborah Feingold; 153: PalmOne Inc.; 154: Getty Images/Ted Thai (left), Getty Images/Justin Sullivan (right); 155: Getty Images/Business Wire; 156: Picture-Desk/Images courtesy of Advertising Archives; 160: www.sandmuseum.com (left), Brookhaven National Laboratory (right); 161: MIT Museum (left), John Robertson/www.flippers.com (right); 162: www.atariarchives.org (bottom right), Getty Images/John Harding/Time Life Pictures (top left); 163: David Winter; 164: Gregory D. George/www.ataritimes.com (top left), René Speranza (right); 165: Picture-Desk/Image courtesy of The Advertising Archives; 166: Moby Games; 167: Picture-Desk/Image courtesy of The Advertising Archives; 168–9: Moby Games; 170: Getty Images/Lucy Nicholson/AFP; 171: Rex Features/Sipa Press; 172: Pepe Tozzo; 172–3: Erik Klooster; 173: Matt Reichert; 174–5: Nintendo/Cake Media PR; 176: Corbis/Roger Ressmeyer; 177: Moby Games (left), Rex Features (right); 178: Picture-Desk/Image courtesy of The Advertising Archives; 179: Getty Images/Joe Raedle; 180: Bandai; 181: Rex Features; 182: Getty Images/Microsoft; 183: Picture-Desk/Image courtesy of The Advertising Archives (left), Corbis/Rick Friedman (right); 184–5: 'Halo 2' courtesy of Xbox Media; 186–7: Corbis/Ed Quinn; 190: Corbis/Reuters; 191: Corbis/Ed Quinn; 192: Empics/AP; 193: Photos12.com/CCETT; 194: Rex Features/Everett Collection; 195: Corbis/Ed Kashi; 196: Courtesy of the author; 197: Private Collection; 198: www.w3.org (left), Corbis/J.L. Atlan (right); 199: Empics/AP; 200: Courtesy of the author; 201: Corbis/Los Angeles Daily News (left), AKG-Images/Ullstein Bild/Joker-Magunia (right); 202: Rex Features; 203: Corbis/Nathaniel Welch; 204–05: Corbis/Tom Grill; 205: Topfoto.co.uk/Norbert Schwerin/The Image Works; 206–07: Picture-Desk/MGM/The Kobal Collection; 210: Rex Features/Everett Collection; 211: Rex Features/Snap; 212: Patte Wood; 213: Topfoto.co.uk/Ann Ronan/HIP; 214: Picture-Desk/The Kobal Collection/20th Century Fox (left), Aquarius Collection/Columbia TriStar/Phoenix (right); 215: Science & Society Picture Library (left), Corbis/Bettmann (right); 216–17: Picture-Desk/MGM/The Kobal Collection; 218–19: Rex Features/Snap; 220: Science & Society Picture Library; 221: Topfoto.co.uk/KPA (top), Rex Features/Everett Collection (bottom); 222: Ronald Grant Archive; 223: Private Collection; 224: Topfoto.co.uk/KPA (left), Rex Features (right); 225: Rex Features/c.Warner Bros./Everett Collection (left). Corbis/Warner Bros. Pictures/Bureau L.A. Collection (right); 226: Private Collection; 227: Courtesy of Apple; 228–9: Science Photo Library/NASA; 232: Lynch Exhibits (left), www.mondolithic.com (right); 233: Gerhard Reitmayr; 234–5: Anti-Gravity Workshop; 236: Rex Features/Andy Paradise; 237: Science Photo Library/Gusto; 238: MacDougall Bio Communications Inc. (left), Ambient Devices (right); 239: Science Photo Library/Volker Steger; 240: Science Photo Library/David Parker; 241: NASA; 242: Science Photo Library/NASA; 243: Corbis/Charles O'Rear; 244: www.eink.com (left), DOE (right); 245: www.scottevest.com (left), Microsoft Research (right); 246: Science Photo Library/David Parker; 246–7: Getty Images/David Friedman; 247: Corbis/Toshiyuki Aizawa; 248–9: www.ifmachines.com; 250–51: Science Photo Library/Peter Menzel; 252: Science Photo Library/Victor Habbick Visions

Book icons designed by simonwilder@shinydesign.com

Special thanks go to the following people: Kevin Davis, Sellam Ismail, Magdalena Mayo, Jenny O'Neil, Anel Rodriguez, Anna-Louise Whitaker and Horst Zuse

Every effort has been made to acknowledge correctly and contact the source and/or copyright holder of each picture, and Carlton Books apologizes for any unintentional errors or omissions, which will be corrected in future editions of this book.